THE
TUNICA-BILOXI

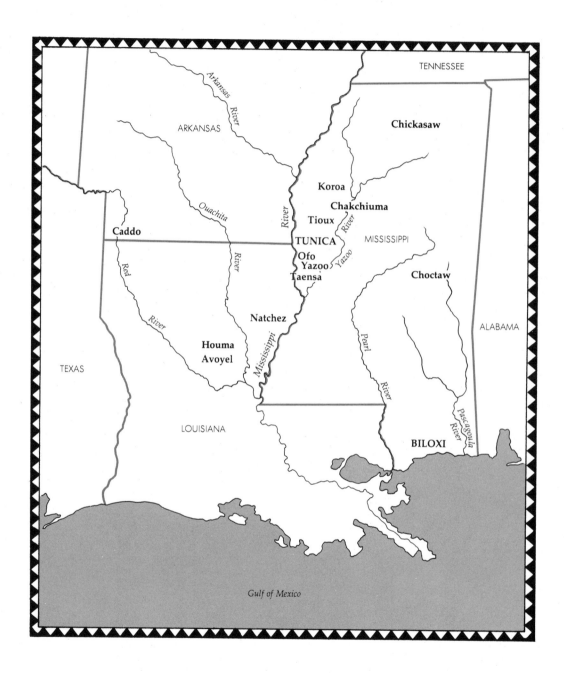

THE
TUNICA-BILOXI

Jeffrey P. Brain

*Curator of Southeastern United States
Archaeology, Peabody Museum,
Harvard University*

Frank W. Porter III
General Editor

CHELSEA HOUSE PUBLISHERS
New York   Philadelphia

On the cover   A clay pot from the Tunica Treasure. The item, made in the mid-1700s, is of Indian manufacture.

Chelsea House Publishers
Editor-in-Chief   Nancy Toff
Executive Editor   Remmel T. Nunn
Managing Editor   Karyn Gullen Browne
Copy Chief   Juliann Barbato
Picture Editor   Adrian G. Allen
Art Director   Maria Epes
Manufacturing Manager   Gerald Levine

Indians of North America
Senior Editor   Liz Sonneborn

Staff for **THE TUNICA-BILOXI**
Associate Editor   Clifford W. Crouch
Deputy Copy Chief   Nicole Bowen
Assistant Art Director   Loraine Machlin
Designer   Donna Sinisgalli
Design Assistant   James Baker
Picture Researcher   Kathryn Bonomi
Production Coordinator   Joseph Romano

First Printing

1 3 5 7 9 8 6 4 2

Library of Congress Cataloging-in-Publication Data

Brain, Jeffrey P.
The Tunica-Biloxi / Jeffrey P. Brain.
   p.   cm.—(Indians of North America)
Bibliography: p.
Includes index.
Summary: Examines the history, changing fortunes, and current status of the Tunica-Biloxi Indians.
ISBN 1-55546-731-8
      0-7910-0399-X (pbk.)
1. Tunica Indians. 2. Biloxi Indians. [1. Tunica Indians. 2. Biloxi Indians. 3. Indians of North America.] I. Title. II. Series: Indians of North America (Chelsea House Publishers)   89-7327
E99.T875B73 1989   CIP
973'.04975—dc20   AC

CONTENTS

INDIANS OF NORTH AMERICA

CHELSEA HOUSE PUBLISHERS

INDIANS OF NORTH AMERICA: CONFLICT AND SURVIVAL

Frank W. Porter III

The Indians survived our open intention of wiping them out, and since the tide turned they have even weathered our good intentions toward them, which can be much more deadly.

John Steinbeck
America and Americans

When Europeans first reached the North American continent, they found hundreds of tribes occupying a vast and rich country. The newcomers quickly recognized the wealth of natural resources. They were not, however, so quick or willing to recognize the spiritual, cultural, and intellectual riches of the people they called Indians.

The Indians of North America examines the problems that develop when people with different cultures come together. For American Indians, the consequences of their interaction with non-Indian people have been both productive and tragic. The Europeans believed they had "discovered" a "New World," but their religious bigotry, cultural bias, and materialistic world view kept them from appreciating and understanding the people who lived in it. All too often they attempted to change the way of life of the indigenous people. The Spanish conquistadores wanted the Indians as a source of labor. The Christian missionaries, many of whom were English, viewed them as potential converts. French traders and trappers used the Indians as a means to obtain pelts. As Francis Parkman, the 19th-century historian, stated, "Spanish civilization crushed the Indian; English civilization scorned and neglected him; French civilization embraced and cherished him."

7

Nearly 500 years later, many people think of American Indians as curious vestiges of a distant past, waging a futile war to survive in a Space Age society. Even today, our understanding of the history and culture of American Indians is too often derived from unsympathetic, culturally biased, and inaccurate reports. The American Indian, described and portrayed in thousands of movies, television programs, books, articles, and government studies, has either been raised to the status of the "noble savage" or disparaged as the "wild Indian" who resisted the westward expansion of the American frontier.

Where in this popular view are the real Indians, the human beings and communities whose ancestors can be traced back to ice-age hunters? Where are the creative and indomitable people whose sophisticated technologies used the natural resources to ensure their survival, whose military skill might even have prevented European settlement of North America if not for devastating epidemics and disruption of the ecology? Where are the men and women who are today diligently struggling to assert their legal rights and express once again the value of their heritage?

The various Indian tribes of North America, like people everywhere, have a history that includes population expansion, adaptation to a range of regional environments, trade across wide networks, internal strife, and warfare. This was the reality. Europeans justified their conquests, however, by creating a mythical image of the New World and its native people. In this myth, the New World was a virgin land, waiting for the Europeans. The arrival of Christopher Columbus ended a timeless primitiveness for the original inhabitants.

Also part of this myth was the debate over the origins of the American Indians. Fantastic and diverse answers were proposed by the early explorers, missionairies, and settlers. Some thought that the Indians were descended from the Ten Lost Tribes of Israel, others that they were descended from inhabitants of the lost continent of Atlantis. One writer suggested that the Indians had reached North America in another Noah's ark.

A later myth, perpetrated by many historians, focused on the relentless persecution during the past five centuries until only a scattering of these "primitive" people remained to be herded onto reservations. This view fails to chronicle the overt and covert ways in which the Indians successfully coped with the intruders.

All of these myths presented one-sided interpretations that ignored the complexity of European and American events and policies. All left serious questions unanswered. What were the origins of the American Indians? Where did they come from? How and when did they get to the New World? What was their life—their culture—really like?

In the late 1800s, anthropologists and archaeologists in the Smithsonian Institution's newly created Bureau of American Ethnology in Washington,

D.C., began to study scientifically the history and culture of the Indians of North America. They were motivated by an honest belief that the Indians were on the verge of extinction and that along with them would vanish their languages, religious beliefs, technology, myths, and legends. These men and women went out to visit, study, and record data from as many Indian communities as possible before this information was forever lost.

By this time there was a new myth in the national consciousness. American Indians existed as figures in the American past. They had performed a historical mission. They had challenged white settlers who trekked across the continent. Once conquered, however, they were supposed to accept graciously the way of life of their conquerors.

The reality again was different. American Indians resisted both actively and passively. They refused to lose their unique identity, to be assimilated into white society. Many whites viewed the Indians not only as members of a conquered nation but also as "inferior" and "unequal." The rights of the Indians could be expanded, contracted, or modified as the conquerors saw fit. In every generation, white society asked itself what to do with the American Indians. Their answers have resulted in the twists and turns of federal Indian policy.

There were two general approaches. One way was to raise the Indians to a "higher level" by "civilizing" them. Zealous missionaries considered it their Christian duty to elevate the Indian through conversion and scanty education. The other approach was to ignore the Indians until they disappeared under pressure from the ever-expanding white society. The myth of the "vanishing Indian" gave stronger support to the latter option, helping to justify the taking of the Indians' land.

Prior to the end of the 18th century, there was no national policy on Indians simply because the American nation has not yet come into existence. American Indians similarly did not possess a political or social unity with which to confront the various Europeans. They were not homogeneous. Rather, they were loosely formed bands and tribes, speaking nearly 300 languages and thousands of dialects. The collective identity felt by Indians today is a result of their common experiences of defeat and/or mistreatment at the hands of whites.

During the colonial period, the British crown did not have a coordinated policy toward the Indians of North America. Specific tribes (most notably the Iroquois and the Cherokee) became military and political pawns used by both the crown and the individual colonies. The success of the American Revolution brought no immediate change. When the United States acquired new territory from France and Mexico in the early 19th century, the federal government wanted to open this land to settlement by homesteaders. But the Indian tribes that lived on this land had signed treaties with European governments assuring their title to the land. Now the United States assumed legal responsibility for honoring these treaties.

At first, President Thomas Jefferson believed that the Louisiana Purchase contained sufficient land for both the Indians and the white population. Within a generation, though, it became clear that the Indians would not be allowed to remain. In the 1830s the federal government began to coerce the eastern tribes to sign treaties agreeing to relinquish their ancestral land and move west of the Mississippi River. Whenever these negotiations failed, President Andrew Jackson used the military to remove the Indians. The southeastern tribes, promised food and transportation during their removal to the West, were instead forced to walk the "Trail of Tears." More than 4,000 men, woman, and children died during this forced march. The "removal policy" was successful in opening the land to homesteaders, but it created enormous hardships for the Indians.

By 1871 most of the tribes in the United States had signed treaties ceding most or all of their ancestral land in exchange for reservations and welfare. The treaty terms were intended to bind both parties for all time. But in the General Allotment Act of 1887, the federal government changed its policy again. Now the goal was to make tribal members into individual landowners and farmers, encouraging their absorption into white society. This policy was advantageous to whites who were eager to acquire Indian land, but it proved disastrous for the Indians. One hundred thirty-eight million acres of reservation land were subdivided into tracts of 160, 80, or as little as 40 acres, and allotted tribe members on an individual basis. Land owned in this way was said to have "trust status" and could not be sold. But the surplus land—all Indian land not allotted to individuals—was opened (for sale) to white settlers. Ultimately, more than 90 million acres of land were taken from the Indians by legal and illegal means.

The resulting loss of land was a catastrophe for the Indians. It was necessary to make it illegal for Indians to sell their land to non-Indians. The Indian Reorganization Act of 1934 officially ended the allotment period. Tribes that voted to accept the provisions of this act were reorganized, and an effort was made to purchase land within preexisting reservations to restore an adequate land base.

Ten years later, in 1944, federal Indian policy again shifted. Now the federal government wanted to get out of the "Indian business." In 1953 an act of Congress named specific tribes whose trust status was to be ended "at the earliest possible time." This new law enabled the United States to end unilaterally, whether the Indians wished it or not, the special status that protected the land in Indian tribal reservations. In the 1950s federal Indian policy was to transfer federal responsibility and jurisdiction to state governments, encourage the physical relocation of Indian peoples from reservations to urban areas, and hasten the termination, or extinction, of tribes.

Between 1954 and 1962 Congress passed specific laws authorizing the termination of more than 100 tribal groups. The stated purpose of the termination policy was to ensure the full and complete integration of Indians into American society. However, there is a less benign way to interpret this legislation. Even as termination was being discussed in Congress, 133 separate bills were introduced to permit the transfer of trust land ownership from Indians to non-Indians.

With the Johnson administration in the 1960s the federal government began to reject termination. In the 1970s yet another Indian policy emerged. Known as "self-determination," it favored keeping the protective role of the federal government while increasing tribal participation in, and control of, important areas of local government. In 1983 President Reagan, in a policy statement on Indian affairs, restated the unique "government is government" relationship of the United States with the Indians. However, federal programs since then have moved toward transferring Indian affairs to individual states, which have long desired to gain control of Indian land and resources.

As long as American Indians retain power, land, and resources that are coveted by the states and the federal government, there will continue to be a "clash of cultures," and the issues will be contested in the courts, Congress, the White House, and even in the international human rights community. To give all Americans a greater comprehension of the issues and conflicts involving American Indians today is a major goal of this series. These issues are not easily understood, nor can these conflicts be readily resolved. The study of North American Indian history and culture is a necessary and important step toward that comprehension. All Americans must learn the history of the relations between the Indians and the federal government, recognize the unique legal status of the Indians, and understand the heritage and cultures of the Indians of North America.

A contemporary artist's conception of Quizquiz, based on archaeological evidence and the chronicles of the de Soto expedition.

THE
PEOPLE
OF
QUIZQUIZ

There stood a mountain, and in the mountain one day a crevice opened up. The Tunica emerged from this. When they had all come forth, they settled nearby. The Tunica lived on the land, and there they hunted.

One day outlanders came to the place from which the Tunica had emerged. The Tunica fought but then stopped, for they did not wish to fight.

And so they went down the Mississippi, until they came to a place where it met another river. There they stopped and settled. A French priest came and dwelt among them. He remained with them for many years.

Then some neighboring peoples joined together. They came and fought the Tunica and killed half of them. The Tunica chief gathered his people together, and once more they traveled down the Mississippi, their big boats tied together. At last the rope broke, and one boat sailed away down the river. The other boat came to rest on the shore. The Tunica settled there.

One night the Tunica held a great feast. Once more some neighboring people came. They all joined in dancing. At midnight they stopped, and the Tunica slept. Without warning, the people attacked them again. Nevertheless, the Tunica drove them away.

In this place the Tunica lived many years. One day the chief sat looking over the water. He spoke to his people. "Land lies to the west," he said. The Tunica left their homes and settled on Prairie Island. The Spanish came to their help during a war. The Spanish gave the land to the Tunica.

Then other people came, took the land, and settled on it. It has now come to pass that the Tunica have scarcely anything. The Tunica are a good people. They have become nearly extinct.

A 1720 drawing by French artist Jean-Baptiste Michel of an Indian settlement at Nouveau Biloxy (New Biloxi), on the Gulf Coast. The Biloxi Indians were to merge with the Tunica tribe over the course of the 19th century.

In this manner do the Tunica Indians give, through a compiling of their own legends, a brief account of their history. When the ancestors of this tribe first came in contact with Europeans, they dwelt along the lower Mississippi River, in what are now the states of Arkansas and Mississippi. During the 17th and 18th centuries, they moved farther downriver in a sequence of migrations. By the end of the 1700s, they had finally settled near the present-day town of Marksville, in central Louisiana. The word *Tunica* (sometimes written as Tonica, Tonnicas, or Thonnicas) translates as ''the people'' and is the tribe's name for itself.

Among the tribes that lived near the Tunica were the Biloxi Indians. The Biloxi first encountered French explorers on the coast of the Gulf of Mexico near present-day Biloxi, Mississippi, in 1699. They, too, migrated during the 18th century and eventually established themselves in the same area of Louisiana as the Tunica. Over the course of the 19th century, the two tribes and remnants of several others, such as the Ofo, Avoyel, and Choctaw, merged. By the 20th century, they had become known as the Tunica-Biloxi. Although the Biloxi are of a different origin and originally spoke a different language, their way of life was similar to that of the Tunica. We can therefore tell the history of the two tribes from a single perspective.

The ancestors of the Tunica first came into contact with Europeans less than 50 years after Christopher Columbus's first voyage across the Atlantic Ocean in 1492. Columbus himself explored only the islands of the Caribbean and, later, the coastline of Central America. It was one of his successors, the Spaniard Juan Ponce de León, who became in 1513 the first European known to lay eyes on the southern shores of what is now the United States. Arriving in this new land at Easter time—in Spanish, *Pascua Florida*—he called it Florida, and for many years the entire Gulf Coast region was known by that name.

In the 1530s, the Spanish explorer Hernando de Soto, who had played a major role in the conquest of Peru, received a commission from the king of Spain to seek out the wealth rumored to lie within the northern continent. Landing on the coast of what is today the state of Florida in May 1539, he proceeded to explore a vast area that included parts of present-day Georgia, South Carolina, North Carolina, Tennessee, Alabama, and Mississippi. After two years he and his soldiers, who were known as *conquistadores*, reached the Mississippi River. There they encountered a settlement identified as Quizquiz.

The chronicles written by various members of the de Soto expedition tell us a great deal about this encounter. According to their accounts, de Soto's soldiers captured more than 300 women from Quizquiz while the men from the settlement were away farming their fields. Among these women was the mother of the *cacique*, the leader of several towns and villages. De Soto sent word of her capture to the cacique, who agreed to meet with the explorer on the condition that she be released.

Exhausted and weak from lack of food and from their long journey, de Soto's men were eager to establish peace with the Indians. They released all their captives and waited for the cacique to arrive the next day. But a large group of Indians carrying bows and arrows came to them instead. De Soto ordered his men to arm themselves and mount their horses in preparation for battle. The Indians stopped their advance "at a distance of a crossbow-shot" from de Soto. After a tense half hour of silence, six chiefs approached. One chronicler of the expedition described the event as follows:

> [The chiefs said] that they had come to find out what people [we] might be; for they had knowledge from their ancestors that they were to be subdued by a white race; they consequently desired to return to the Cacique, to tell him that he should come presently to obey and serve the Governor [that is, de Soto]. After presenting six or seven skins and shawls brought with them, they took their leave, and returned with the others who were waiting for them by the shore. The Cacique came not, nor sent another message.

The Indians in the immediate area had a small food supply, so the starving soldiers soon moved to another town nearby that had enjoyed a large harvest of corn. They then established a camp there and began to build barges, on which they planned to continue their journey. Soon another group of Indians approached and told them that their cacique, Aquixo, and his people wished to meet with de Soto the following day.

This time the cacique did arrive, along with 200 canoes filled with warriors. A Spanish eyewitness later described the meeting:

> They were painted with ochre [red and yellow pigment], wearing great bunches of white and other plumes of many colors, having feathered shields in their hands, with which they sheltered the oarsmen on either side, the warriors standing erect from bow to stern, holding bows and arrows. . . . [The] Cacique said to the Governor, who was walking along the river-bank, with others who bore him company, that he had come to visit, serve, and obey him; for he had heard that he was the greatest of lords, the most powerful on all the earth, and that he must see what he would have him do. The Governor expressed his pleasure, and besought him to land, that they might the better confer; but the Chief gave no reply, ordering three barges to draw near, wherein was great quantity of fish, and loaves like bricks, made of the pulp of ameixas [persimmons], which De Soto receiving, gave him thanks and again entreated him to land.
> Making the gift had been a pretext, to discover if any harm might be done; but, finding the Governor and his people on their guard, the Cacique began to draw off from the shore, when the crossbow-men, who were in readiness, with loud cries shot at the Indians, and struck down five or six of them. They retired with great order, not one leaving the oar, even though the one next to him might have fallen, and covering themselves, they withdrew. Afterwards they came many times and landed; when approached, they would go back to their barges. These were fine-looking men, very large and well formed; and what with the awnings, the plumes, and the shields, the pennons [flags], and the number of people in the fleet, it appeared like a famous armada of galleys.

According to a chronicler, after this incident, "the Indians every day, at three o'clock in the afternoon, would get into two hundred and fifty very large canoes they had, well shielded, and come near the shore on which we were; with loud cries they would exhaust their arrows upon us, and then return to the other bank. . . . But when they saw that work on the barges did not relax on their account, they said that Pacaha, whose men they were, ordered them to withdraw, and so they left the passage free."

The observations of de Soto's men help us to reconstruct the world of these ancestors of the Tunica. We know from these sources that 16th-century Quizquiz had a highly organized society, comprising many towns and villages, and was inhabited by thousands of

Hernando de Soto, leader of the first expedition of Europeans to encounter the Tunica's ancestors. The original caption to this drawing notes that he "went through la Florida [the Gulf Coast] and defeated the natives, invincible until then."

people. De Soto's chroniclers were told that the people of Quizquiz were the subjects of Aquixo, who was in turn the subject of yet another leader (identified both as Pacaha and Capaha). This suggests that a political hierarchy existed in the region that extended even beyond Quizquiz.

The many towns of Quizquiz appear to have been ranked in importance, a grading probably indicated by the number of monumental earthworks constructed in each settlement. These mounds, often 30 to 40 feet high and supported by embankments, served as foundations for temples and the houses of caciques. They elevated these structures in a way that emphasized their social importance. They may also have had some connection to a sun-based religion practiced by the people, though the particulars of this are uncertain.

The remains of these settlements (which we now refer to as *mound sites*) and their cemeteries attest to both the large population and the complex social, political, and religious development of Quizquiz. Though they are impressive, these physical artifacts tell us little about the organization of the

A sketch by the author of the first confrontation between the warriors of Quizquiz and Hernando de Soto's soldiers.

society itself, however. For much of that information one must rely on the de Soto chronicles.

From them we know that Quizquiz had an abundance of food. Specifically, they mention that the Indians had large supplies of maize (Indian corn), fish, persimmons, and pecans. The fertile land along the Mississippi River supported a great variety of animal and vegetable life, and the people of Quizquiz supplemented the food that they obtained by fishing, hunting, and gathering by growing their own crops, including squash, beans, and pumpkins. Their surplus food was not only a godsend to the starving conquistadores but also a testimonial to the thriving tribal economy.

It appears from the de Soto chronicles that the men of Quizquiz, rather than the women, were responsible for the cultivation of the fields—a division of labor demonstrating their commitment to agriculture. (In many neighboring tribes, the men hunted, and the women gathered wild foodstuffs.) It is likely that each man served in more than one social role—acting as both soldier and farmer, for example—but, again, current knowledge is uncertain.

Other aspects of this society are mentioned only fleetingly in the chronicles. From these documents we know that Quizquiz possessed a fleet of large canoes, each manned by up to 80 rowers and warriors, which apparently worked in cooperation with the fleets of their Indian allies. All accounts state that de Soto's soldiers took skins, shawls, and other clothing in their initial assault, but this indicates little except that the Indians made such objects. The only other items at Quizquiz that the Spaniards described were those that threatened them: canoes, bows and arrows, and other instruments of war.

Archaeologists have excavated these objects from Quizquiz sites dating from the time of the de Soto expedition. However, the artifacts that best characterize the encounter between de Soto and Quizquiz are not weapons. They are little brass bells called Clarksdale bells, so named after the present-day town of Clarksdale, Mississippi, where many have been recovered. De Soto used these both as tokens of friendship and as trade items with which to acquire the essentials of survival. Another possible de Soto relic, a distinctive type of halberd (battle-ax), has also been found in the vicinity. Other probable artifacts of the expedition—such as glass beads (also used as tokens of friendship) and parts of swords and matchlock guns—have been found just west of the Mississippi River.

The 16th-century domain visited briefly by de Soto was physically characterized by large, permanent towns with monumental earthworks. Its populace was divided essentially into the common people and the elite, which comprised religious leaders, chiefs, and seasoned warriors. (The distinction between these two groups is established both by differing methods of burial and by objects buried as religious offerings in certain graves.) The mass of warriors, which numbered in the thousands, served under secondary chiefs, who in turn united in alliance under a preeminent chief.

Many of these attributes were shared by other southeastern peoples. What stands out about Quizquiz is its size, which suggests a surprisingly complex society. The development of Quizquiz was made possible by its rich environment and, equally important,

A contemporary map showing the location of the village and mounds of Quizquiz in relation to the streets of downtown Clarksdale, Mississippi, the town that now occupies this former Indian site.

by its location. Large amounts of food could have been obtained elsewhere in the region, but only by settling on the banks of the Mississippi River could the tribe travel with ease to many other villages by canoe. The Mississippi is the great central waterway of North America, and many lesser rivers flow into it. The location of Quizquiz on its banks fostered contact and trade, initially with other tribes and ultimately with European explorers and immigrants.

By comparison with their previous encounters with other Indian tribes, the travel-wearied conquistadores inflicted little bloodshed upon the people of Quizquiz. But the Spaniards did kill or enslave some of the natives, disrupt the existing social order, and, in all likelihood, exhaust the area's food supply. As they remained in the region a month, and undoubtedly needed extra food with which to continue their expedition, it is probable that they pirated all the provisions of Quizquiz and depleted the immediate area of natural foodstuffs as well. Although the river valley was rich in resources, the loss of their own food reserves must have been a calamity to the Quizquiz population.

Considering the length of the expedition's stay, an even greater danger to the natives was the possibility of contracting European diseases. Many diseases common in Europe were completely new to the Indians. Because they had not developed immunity to such diseases, they were extraordinarily vulnerable to them. For many years after first contact, the native population

of North America fell drastically as Indians across the continent died in epidemics of smallpox, measles, and other diseases previously unknown to them.

It is doubtful, however, that de Soto's expedition was an immediate villain in this respect. His army was small and seems to have had little contact with the natives of Quizquiz. Yet the expedition, surely a traumatic event to the Indians in itself, was at least a harbinger of the scourge. Although there are no records of direct contact between the inhabitants of Quizquiz and Europeans again for more than 100 years, the events that occurred during the century following de Soto's visit were clearly catastrophic to the Indian settlement.

During that dark age, epidemic disease struck. On the Atlantic and Gulf coasts, European colonial settlements that included children (who are great incubators of germs) must have spread disease rapidly among nearby natives. In turn, the Indians' trade routes became avenues of death, as coastal Indian traders carried the diseases to groups farther inland. The Mississippi River, that great central artery, would have been one of the worst of all. Contact among tribes along the Mississippi was rapid, constant, and far reaching, all factors that would lead to rampant spread of disease. The concentration of people in Quizquiz could only add to the severity of the results, which must have been disastrous.

Famine was an immediate outcome. After epidemic disease and death struck

View of the Lower Mississippi, *painted in the 1830s by George Catlin, American artist and observer of Indian life. The Mississippi has played a crucial role throughout Tunica history as both a source of sustenance and an avenue of trade.*

a commmunity, crops would consequently either lie in the fields untended and unharvested or else never get planted at all. The hunt had to be abandoned, and the gathering of wild foods neglected. In short, all of the Indians' traditional ways of obtaining food were disrupted.

It is likely that the epidemics brought about the collapse of social and political order as well, as many leaders died from disease. This in turn may have led to war among tribes, with remnants of peoples struggling for control of their land and that of their neighbors.

Whatever happened, the relatively well developed political and social structures of Quizquiz witnessed by de Soto in the mid-1500s ceased to exist. After this complete collapse, brought on by decreases in town and village populations as great as 70 to 80 percent, the remaining people regrouped and moved away from the scene of so much horror. When French explorers arrived at the Mississippi River at the end of the 17th century, they found the survivors of this chain of events. Among them was a group of Indians known as the Tunica. ▲

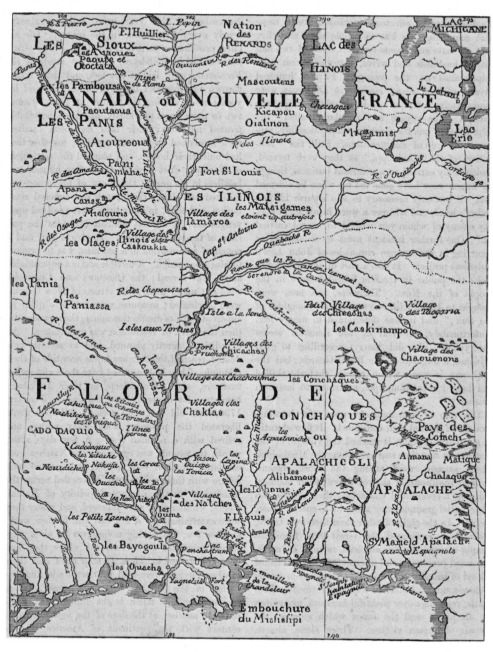

A French map from 1703 showing the course of the Mississippi River. The Tunica (here identified as les Tonica) would become valuable allies and trading partners of the French in Louisiana.

ALONG THE
YAZOO RIVER

In the late 17th century, Tunica territory once again came under European influence. In 1673, two Frenchmen—Louis Jolliet, a fur trader and explorer, and Father Jacques Marquette, a Catholic priest of the Jesuit order (Society of Jesus)—led an expedition that opened up the Mississippi River valley to the French. Their main purpose, however, was simply to find into which ocean, Atlantic or Pacific, the river ran. Starting from settlements in Canada, the small party canoed down the Mississippi as far as its junction with the Arkansas River. At that point, Jolliet and Marquette decided to return upriver. Having satisfied themselves that the river fed into the Gulf of Mexico, they feared they might run into hostile Indian or Spanish forces by continuing south.

Nine years later, French explorer René-Robert Cavelier, sieur de La Salle,

traveled down the Mississippi all the way to its mouth at the Gulf of Mexico. La Salle claimed the entire river valley for France and named the new territory Louisiana in honor of his king, Louis XIV. For the next 80 years the French would maintain their claim to the region by settling and developing their new colony.

At the time of the La Salle expedition, the Tunica lived in the region of the Yazoo River, in what is now northwestern Mississippi. La Salle never explored the Yazoo, and a permanent French settlement was not established in the area until the end of the 17th century. The first recorded contact between the French and the Tunica occurred in 1699, when a group of missionaries from the Séminaire de Québec in Canada visited the tribe. Renewed relations with Europeans brought more disease to the Indians

Jacques Marquette and Louis Jolliet exploring the Mississippi River in 1673. The members of this expedition were the first Europeans to journey through the Southeast since de Soto's foray into the region more than a century earlier.

who had survived the earlier epidemics. The total native population of the Yazoo River region dropped from several thousand to a few hundred in a brief time. Eventually, however, the number of deaths leveled off. Epidemics would continue to break out occasionally, but from this time on European influence would be more cultural than biological.

The Tunica in 1699 were far removed from their Quizquiz ancestors both geographically and culturally. But their way of life was still essentially unaffected by European customs. The

writings of two Frenchmen, J.-B. La Source and Father Jacques Gravier, are the source of practically all we know about the Tunica before prolonged contact with Europeans changed them irrevocably. La Source, a layman, accompanied the Quebec missionaries in 1699, and Gravier visited the Tunica in November 1700. Thus both were on the scene at the very outset of French contact with the tribe. Fortunately, both also appear to have been keen and reliable observers.

According to La Source, the French missionaries estimated the Indian population of the lower Yazoo River region in 1699 (before the epidemics) to be approximately 2,000, of which the Tunica probably made up slightly more than half. The remaining people belonged to at least four smaller tribes, including the Yazoo, Ofo, Koroa, and Tioux. Unlike the latter groups, which had dispersed into small settlements, the Tunica had one principal village. It has been identified as the one excavated at the present-day archaeological site of Haynes Bluff, Mississippi.

The importance of this village to the Tunica is confirmed by the presence of four mounds. The highest of them rises to approximately 33 feet and probably once supported a temple. Excavations

(continued on page 28)

La Salle and Father Hennepin on the Mississippi, *from a sketch by Hennepin, published in 1683. The priest was one of the many missionaries who introduced Christianity and French culture to southeastern Indians.*

DELUGE AND DEATH
ON THE MISSISSIPPI

The Mississippi River has been vital to the Tunica throughout recorded history, providing food, transportation, communication, and an avenue of trade. But with the river's benefits historically came hazards, chiefly its catastrophic floods. The following is an account of the great spring flood of 1882; its backdrop is the junction of the Mississippi and Red rivers near Avoyelles (now Marksville, Louisiana), where the Tunica settled in the early 1800s. The report, detailing the voyage of a steamboat bringing supplies to survivors, is taken from Life on the Mississippi, *published in 1883, by American author Mark Twain (1835–1910).*

"It was nine o'clock Thursday morning when the [steamboat] 'Susie' left the Mississippi and entered the Old River, or what is now called the mouth of the Red. Ascending on the left, a flood was pouring in through and over the levees on the Chandler plantation, the most northern point in Point Coupée parish. The water covered the place, although the levees had given way but a short time before.

"The woods look bright and fresh, but this pleasant aspect to the eye is neutralized by the interminable waste of water. We pass mile after mile, and it is nothing but trees standing up to their branches in water. A water-turkey [a local species of bird] now and again rises and flies ahead into the long avenues of silence.

"One man, whom your correspondent spoke to, said that he had one hundred and fifty head of cattle and one hundred head of hogs. At the first appearance of the water he had started to drive them to the high ground of Avoyelles . . . but he lost fifty head of the beef cattle and sixty hogs.

"Presently a little girl, not over twelve years, paddled out in the smallest little canoe and handled it with all the deftness of an old voyageur. The little one looked more like an Indian than a white child, and laughed when asked if she was afraid. She had been raised in a pirogue [canoe] and could go anywhere. She was bound out to pick willow leaves for the [live]stock, and she pointed to a house near by with water three inches deep on the floors. At its back door was moored a raft about thirty feet square, with a sort of fence built on it, and inside [stood] some sixteen cows and twenty hogs.

"Everything is quiet—the quiet of dissolution. Down the river floats now . . . a bloated carcass, solemnly guarded by a pair of buzzards, the only bird to be seen, which feast on the carcass as it bears them along.

"At two o'clock the 'Susie' reached [the community of] Troy. . . . [The town] is situated on and around three large Indian mounds, circular in shape, which rise above the present water about twelve feet. They are about one hundred and fifty feet in diameter and are about two hundred yards apart. The houses are all built between these mounds, and hence all are flooded.

"These elevations, built by the aborigines hundreds of years ago, are the only point of refuge for miles. When we arrived we found them crowded with [live]stock, all of which was thin and hardly able to stand up. They were mixed together, sheep, hogs, horses, mules, and cattle. One of these mounds has been used for many years as a grave-yard, and to-day we saw attenuated cows lying against the marble tomb-stones.

"The remarkable tenacity of the people here to their homes is beyond all comprehension. . . . After weeks of privation and suffering, people still cling to their houses and leave only when there is not room between the water and the ceiling to build a scaffold on which to stand. . . . Love for the old place [is] stronger than that for safety."

The Mississippi River, in a contemporary photograph, overflows its low-lying banks.

(continued from page 25)

at the summit of this mound have revealed the remains of a structure, and the four mounds are arranged around an open plaza, which may have served as a ceremonial center. Temple mounds such as those found at Haynes Bluff had been constructed by many prehistoric peoples, whom we now call Mississippians. The Tunica seem to have been among the last—perhaps even *the* last—of the mound builders and users.

Little information survives about Tunica beliefs, language, and folklore in the records of early European observers. This is probably because the Tunica's ways were similar to those of neighboring tribes and therefore did not provoke any special attention from French visitors. Father Gravier did note that the Tunica were "very docile." By this he most likely meant that they had few traditions that were offensive to the missionaries and were consequently propitious subjects for religious instruction. Yet the priests no doubt disapproved of some of the tribe's ways. Some Tunica men had more than one wife, and divorce was too easily achieved for the priests' tastes: A man ended his marriage simply by publicly renouncing it (a practice unheard of, however, among the women). The missionaries noted that the Tunica women were generally shy in public and were not so "loose or bold," in Gravier's words, as females of some nearby tribes.

The Tunica also spoke a language very different from those of their Indian neighbors, indicating that they were intruders in the region. This language, known as Tunican, was the only one in the lower Mississippi valley region to have an *r* sound, and it was one of the very few Indian languages with gender distinctions in its grammar. Father Antoine Davion, who established the first mission in Tunica territory in 1699, found the language especially difficult to learn, but this may have been because he was old and not much of a linguist.

Details are even sketchier about the Tunica's political and social structure. Some French records contain references to the Tunica having more than one chief at a time. It is known that at a later period they, like many other southeastern tribes, had one chief for civil affairs and another for war. The civil chief had more influence, and a strong individual may have even assumed both roles on occasion. Early French visitors do not explain how the chiefs obtained their political authority, but later historical documents and Tunica traditions indicate that chiefs inherited their position.

The Tunica told the missionaries little about their religious beliefs and practices. Gravier noted that "they are so close-mouthed as to all the mysteries of their religion that [Davion] could not discover anything about it." Nevertheless, the curious Gravier was able to learn that the Tunica acknowledged nine gods: the sun; thunder; fire; the gods of the east, north, south, and

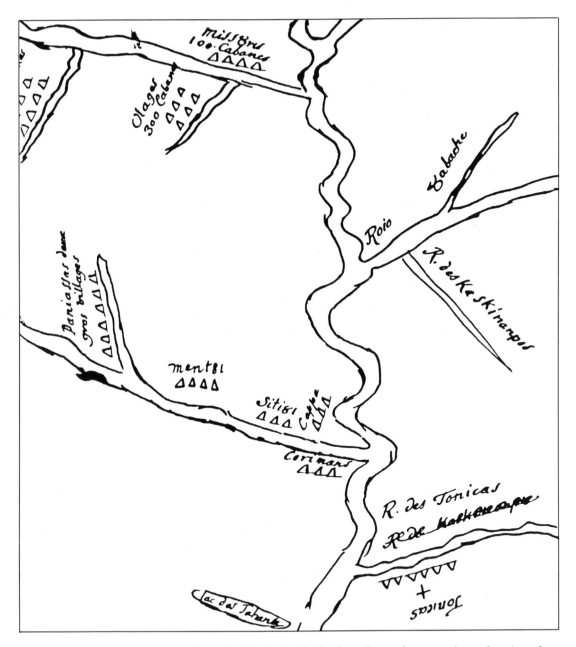

This map, drawn by a priest from the Séminaire de Québec, shows the approximate location of the Tunica and other tribes along the Yazoo River delta in 1698. Missionaries made their first recorded contact with the Tunica the following year.

west; and those of heaven and earth. Apparently, the sun was the foremost of the nine.

The worship of many gods is common among tribes of the southeast. However, fragments of the tribe's an-cient stories suggest several features unique to the Tunica's religious beliefs. Unlike other tribes in the region, they believed that the sun-god was feminine and that fire was a god itself rather than merely a symbol of the sun.

A Tunica frog effigy, which probably symbolized the underworld. Although the Tunica embraced some elements of Christianity, they maintained many of their traditional beliefs for generations after European contact.

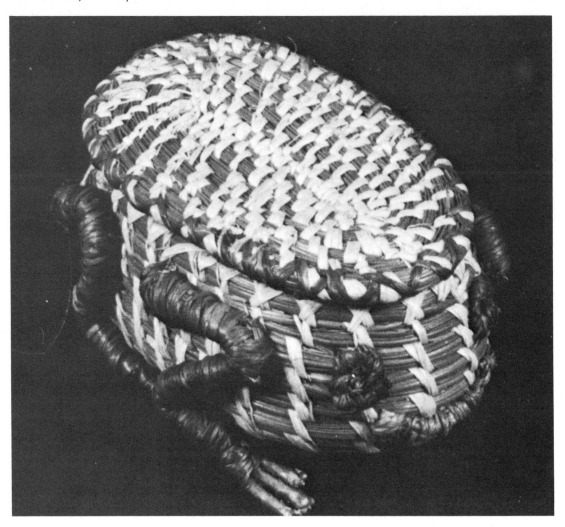

In their temple, the Tunica maintained a fire that was the focus of their religious activities. The temple also housed earthen figures, including effigies of a woman and of a frog. The woman probably symbolized the sun, and the frog perhaps represented the underworld. It is recorded by André Pénicaut, a ship's carpenter and a chronicler of the period, that Father Davion stole into the temple one night and smashed some of the figures and carried away the rest. He escaped without retribution because of the Tunica's high regard for him.

Almost 20 years later, after Davion had left his mission, another visitor, Father Pierre François Xavier de Charlevoix, reported that Davion had set the temple on fire and that the Tunica had never bothered to rebuild it because of their "indifference with respect to religion." However, Charlevoix's account of this, especially his comment on the Tunica's religious apathy, is suspect. It is probable that the earlier report is closer to the truth. In any event, although the Tunica respected Davion and accepted his religious instruction, his baptisms, and even his more zealous deeds, they probably did not significantly change their established beliefs.

Evidence that the Tunica retained many of their beliefs can be found in their burial practices, which the tribe would continue to maintain for many generations to come. La Source stated that "they inter their dead and the relations come to weep with those of the house, and in the evening they weep over the grave of the departed and make a fire there and pass their hands over it, crying out and weeping." Bodies were buried outstretched and face-up, usually in graves lined with bark. The head of the corpse was generally pointed eastward.

Graves were often dug near or even inside the house of the deceased. An assortment of personal items, both ornamental and useful, were almost always buried with the body as religious offerings. Both European goods and objects made by the Indians have been found in gravesites from this period. Father Gravier noted that the Tunica carried all of their personal possessions with them in life. Apparently, the same was true in death.

According to French documents, the Tunica looked much like their neighbors. Gravier reported that the heads of infants were compressed in the cradle in order to flatten the skull; a board was tied across the forehead to push it back, producing what the Tunica considered a countenance of distinction and beauty. But there is no archaeological evidence to support his contention, and this flattening is not depicted in the only known French drawing of Tunica Indians from the early 18th century. All Tunica let their hair grow long. Women arranged theirs in one heavy braid that hung down their back to their waist or in a crown around their head. Both men and women tattooed themselves—generally on the face and sometimes all over the body:

first the arms and legs and perhaps then the torso as well. These tattoos may have served as marks of ancestry, and possibly some had religious significance. Warriors' tattoos denoted their military exploits. Women also blackened their teeth with charcoal, for beauty's sake.

Like other tribes of the lower Mississippi Valley, the Tunica wore very little. Women dressed in short fringed skirts, which were usually of a cloth made from the inner bark of the mulberry tree. Men wore deerskin loincloths, and children went naked. In cold weather, both sexes wore mantles made of mulberry cloth, turkey feathers, or muskrat skins. The Indians also ornamented themselves with shell pendants, beads, and earpins. The last of these were probably worn by women only.

Among the objects manufactured by the Tunica were pottery and stone tools. Gravier noted "earthen pots quite well made, especially little glazed pitchers, as neat as you would see in France." Unlike neighboring tribes— such as the Chickasaw to the northeast, the Choctaw to the southeast, the Natchez to the south, and the Caddo to the west—the Tunica added crushed mussel shell to the clay they used to make their pottery. The mixture made their ceramic works particularly durable. The forms and decorations used by the Tunica also distinguish their pottery.

The Tunica probably also used triangular stone arrow points, which were common among their neighbors to the north but not among the Natchez and most other tribes to the south. It is difficult to say much with certainty about the early Tunica's use of stone tools, for these were rapidly replaced by European metal tools and firearms after the arrival of the French; the Indians obtained them through trade. As early as 1700, Gravier wrote that metal hatchets, kettles, and guns were common Tunica possessions. Remains of these and similar European objects, both functional and decorative, have been found at Tunica sites along the Yazoo.

The only example archaeologists have found of Tunica architecture from this period is the burned structure on the summit of the large mound at Haynes Bluff. The remains reveal few details about the structure's size, form, or function. Gravier did, however, leave a description of typical Tunica dwellings:

> Their cabins are round and vaulted. They are lathed with canes and plastered with mud from bottom to top, within and without with a good covering of straw. There is no light except by the door, and no matter how little fire there is (the smoke of which has no escape but the door) it is as hot as a vapour bath. At night a lighted torch of dried canes serves as a candle and keeps all the cabin warm.

La Source added that "their houses are made of palisades [rows of stakes or canes] and earth, and are very large."

(continued on page 41)

THE TUNICA TREASURE

The Tunica Treasure is a vast and extraordinary collection of objects, made by Europeans and Indians alike, that date from 1731 to 1764, the years the tribe resided at Tunica Bayou, in present-day Louisiana. These artifacts were unearthed in the late 1960s, when a treasure hunter despoiled a graveyard in which the objects had been buried.

The collection is notable not only for its Tunica-made items, such as pottery, but also for the evidence it gives of the sustained, extensive trade between the tribe and its French neighbors. Among the recovered artifacts are ceramic vessels (made by Europeans, Tunica, and other Indian peoples), metal kettles, ax and hoe heads, jewelry, beads, gun parts, and basketry. These demonstrate the cultural flexibility that allowed the Tunica to survive—and, indeed, sometimes thrive on—contact with Europeans.

Many of the objects reveal the influence of European styles. Yet they also show the persistence of traditional Indian materials and designs. Although the Tunica came to use French vessel shapes, they continued their longtime practice of kneading crushed shells into the wet clay so as to strengthen the finished product.

Many of the intricate patterns of traditional Tunica basketwork have also survived. Tribeswomen have continued to handweave such baskets, using longleaf pine needles and other plant fibers, up to the present time.

This bottle may have been made by Tunica along the Ouachita River, or may possibly have been made by Natchez, then acquired by trade.

This mug was made in Germany for sale in England, then was apparently traded to the Tunica by the French. The "GR" stands for Georgius Rex, or King George III of Britain.

This pot's shape is typical of those predating French contact.

The shape of the Tunica pot at left reveals the influence of French vessels, such as the one beside it. Unlike the French, however, the Tunica did not apply glaze to their pottery.

Nearly 200,000 glass beads such as these were discovered as part of the Tunica Treasure. The French often traded beads to the Tunica.

Silver earrings, such as these from the mid-1700s, were popular among the Tunica. The tribe was also eager to trade for bracelets and other ornaments made of copper and brass.

Bells of cast brass, probably made by the English. Bells were popular trade items as far back as the 16th century.

Ear pins made from shell. The Tunica wore such traditional ornaments even after they had obtained European jewelry.

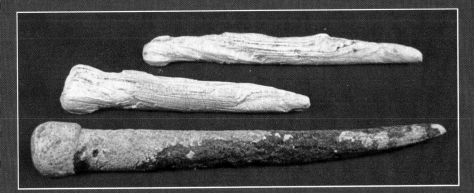

37

Iron ax heads, probably of French manufacture. Such items, acquired by the Tunica in trade, were invaluable to tribal prosperity.

The many iron hoe heads found at Tunica Bayou confirm the tribe's commitment to agriculture.

Brass side plates from a French rifle. The Tunica needed guns primarily for hunting but sometimes used them in combat.

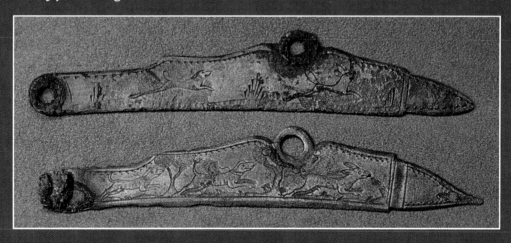

A French-made porringer—a low-sided serving bowl—made of pewter. Bowls such as this have been found only at Tunica Bayou, demonstrating the site's preeminence as a trade center.

A remnant of basketwork from the Tunica Treasure. As the items below show, 20th-century Tunica still make baskets using the same techniques employed by their ancestors.

A split-cane basket that was handwoven in Marksville, Louisiana, in the 1930s.

This fruit basket was handwoven out of pine needles by Anna Mae Juneau of Marksville.

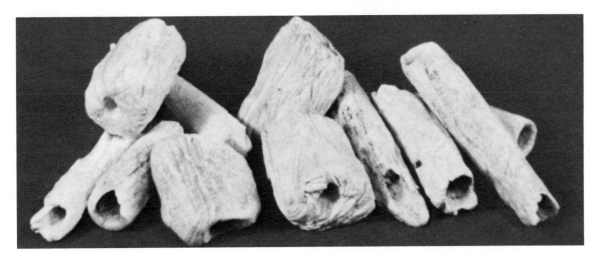

Shell beads, which were worn as pendants by Tunica women and men. Women also wore ear pins made of shell.

(continued from page 32)

The dwellings were built by the wattle-and-daub method common in structures made in the late prehistoric southeast. After planting wooden posts in the ground to form the outline of a dwelling, they wove cane (wattle) horizontally between the posts to make walls, which were then plastered with clay (daub). Just outside their houses they built hearths for cooking and storehouses for grain. Gravier noted that these were "built on four large posts 15 or 16 feet high, well put together, and well polished, so that the mice cannot climb up."

In these granaries the Tunica kept their corn and squash. Gravier judged their crops to be of better quality and more abundant than those of the Illinois tribe to the north, with whom he had spent some time. Both Gravier and La Source observed that the Tunica's cornstalks were 15 to 20 feet high and that their sunflowers, which they raised for the seeds, grew to the same height. The two Frenchmen do not mention beans, but it may be presumed that they were a common food, as neighboring tribes grew them.

Domesticated crops were essentials in the diet of the Tunica and their neighbors as well. But the Tunica's agricultural practices probably differed from those of nearby tribes. La Source wrote that men were "employed solely on their fields, they do not hunt." Gravier was more explicit: "The men do here what peasants do in France; they cultivate and dig the earth, plant and harvest the crops." Such assertions echo the passage in the de Soto chronicles stating that the men of the tribe left their village to tend crops. The Tunica may have been the only eastern tribe in which men had the primary responsibility for working the fields.

Like other southeastern tribes, however, the Tunica also helped themselves to the wild vegetable and animal life that flourished in the Mississippi Valley, especially in the delta where the Yazoo and Mississippi rivers joined. The orange-yellow fruit of the persimmon tree, which the Tunica called *piakimina*, was one of the tribe's most important wild foods. The Tunica dried these fruits and then pounded them into a flour. They baked this into a bread that stayed edible for a long period of time. They also gathered berries, roots, herbs, seeds, nuts, plums, and other fruits.

Despite La Source's claim, the Tunica did hunt. Deer and bear meat was an important part of the Tunica diet. Smaller animals such as squirrels, rabbits, raccoons, and possums were also eaten, as were fish and birds. Buffalo were rare in the Yazoo region, but Tunica expeditions traveled west of the Mississippi probably once a year to hunt small herds that roamed as far afield as the more wooded areas of northern Louisiana.

The Tunica also undertook expeditions for reasons other than obtaining food. According to even the earliest French accounts, the Tunica were actively involved in the production and trade of salt. At the time of first European contact, the Tunica probably drew upon natural deposits formed by salt

The similarity between this glazed jug made by a Tunica in the 1700s and the vessel in this painting, Fruit, Jug, and a Glass *by French artist Jean-Baptiste Siméon Chardin (1699–1779), shows how the tribe's artisans were influenced by European styles.*

The Ouachita River, a tributary of the Mississippi. The Tunica obtained salt, an invaluable trade item, from hot springs along the Ouachita.

springs along the upper Ouachita River in what is now Arkansas; they may also have killed buffalo that were drawn to the salt licks. (Indeed, the presence of salt nearby may even have been the original reason that the ancestors of the Tunica had made the area their homeland.)

Used to season food, salt is dietarily necessary for the healthy functioning of the human body, but it was not easy for some inland tribes to obtain. In carrying it to them, the Tunica performed a vital social function. Its availability to the Tunica gave them a significant trade advantage with these peoples. Their ac-

cess to salt also gave the tribe an advantage over other Indians in dealing with the pioneering French. By the early 1700s, the Tunica had learned to exploit the naturally occurring Louisiana salt domes. Ultimately, this trade probably became an important factor in their survival.

However, trade also put the Tunica in an awkward position. From the outset of their first steady contact with Europeans, they were allies of the French, supplying them with both foodstuffs and salt. Yet there were other Europeans on the scene. Traders from British colonies, such as Georgia and the Car-

Boeuf Sauvage.

A 1758 drawing of an American bison, an animal occasionally hunted by Tunica expeditions. The bison was a novelty to colonists, and the artist, Antoine Simon Le Page du Pratz, identifies it as boeuf sauvage, *or a "savage bull."*

olinas on the Atlantic Coast, already re-sided among the Chickasaw and had long dealt with the Yazoo Indians. In the Yazoo River region, the end point of trading routes originating in Charleston, the British were interested primarily in obtaining from the Indians the high-value items of the so-called skin trade: deerskins and human slaves.

Historical documents indicate that the Tunica were never very active in this trade, and archaeologists confirm that they owned no stone tools appropriate to working deerskin. Whether out of disinclination or allegiance to the French, the Tunica generally refused to trade with the English. But the location of their homeland, squarely between the farthest outposts of the two European powers, made their trade network extraordinarily vulnerable to the growing French-English rivalry in eastern North America.

After several years of conflict, the English brought about the expulsion of the uncooperative Tunica from the Yazoo region in 1706. In that year, the Tunica had captured an English slave trader. After they released him, the trader incited the Chickasaw and other English-allied tribes to take revenge. But the Tunica preempted their attacks by moving farther south, where they would be closer to French settlements. There they had already established satisfactory trade relations, which were becoming fundamental to the tribe's survival. The Tunica's entrepreneurial importance and their reputation as a settled, peaceful tribe ensured that they would be welcome; France was less concerned with the skin trade than with the very survival of Louisiana itself.

The Tunica's alliance with the French would become increasingly important—and ultimately, crucial—to the tribe. Although the missionaries had little initial success in spreading their faith, they—particularly Father Davion, who had lived among the tribe—had helped to attach the Tunica resolutely to their country. This loyalty, which in 1706 parted them from their Yazoo homeland, would have an enormous effect on the tribe over the remainder of the century. ▲

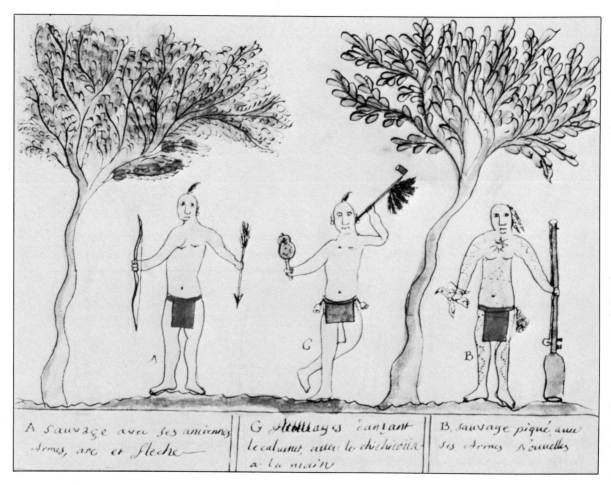

This drawing from around 1730 by French colonist François Dumont de Montigny depicts Louisiana Indians in war and peace. Figure A holds a bow and arrow, traditional Indian weapons; figure B bears a gun of European manufacture; and figure C dances with a calumet (peace pipe) and rattle.

PORTAGE DE LA CROIX

When the Tunica left the Yazoo River region in 1706, they chose to move south. Again they selected a spot on the banks of the Mississippi River, near its junction with a major tributary—this time the Red River. There the Mississippi flowed in a great double loop. The narrow neck of land this loop surrounded was a well-known *portage* (a land route between two bodies of water; in this case, one that interrupts the path of a waterway). The area had been marked with a cross at its southern tip by an early French explorer, Pierre Le Moyne, sieur d'Iberville, and was therefore known as the Portage de la Croix (Path of the Cross).

The Tunica's new location enabled them both to control access to the Red River and to monitor the travelers on the Mississippi who used the portage to cut their travel time. The area was thus doubly attractive to Tunica traders.

In this position, they could continue to trade with other Indian tribes and also take advantage of increased opportunities to deal with the French, who would begin to develop their colony in the lower Mississippi Valley during the second decade of the 18th century. Because the Tunica's new homeland was as hospitable and rich in natural resources as the Yazoo region, the Tunica continued to flourish.

At Portage de la Croix, the tribe arranged its villages as it had done in its Yazoo River home, although its population may have been slightly more concentrated in its new location. The principal village, called Tonicas or Grand Tonicas, was bounded by satellite settlements known as Petits Tonicas (Little Tonicas). These were strategically located at the southern and northern ends of the portage, near the union of the Red and Mississippi rivers.

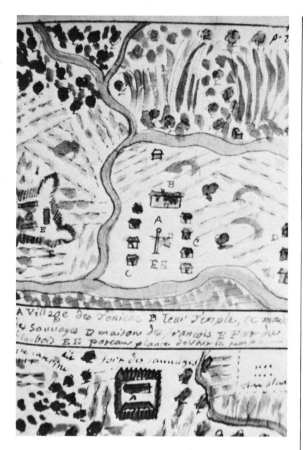

François Dumont de Montigny's map of a Tunica village about 1730 is evidence of the tribe's intimacy with the French colonists. Directly to the right of the Tunica's village are the maisons des Français, *or "homes of the French."*

The principal village had been captured from another tribe, the Houma, who subsequently moved downriver (where they remain to this day). It was situated on a bluff in the middle of the portage. Historical accounts describe the village as rows of houses, 2 or 3 deep, that encompassed the bluff and

surrounded a central plaza that was 100 paces in diameter. Father Charlevoix reported that some houses were square and others round. This was a change from the Tunica's previous settlements, in which, according to Gravier, all of the tribe's houses had been round. (An early-18th-century sketch by François Dumont de Montigny, a colonist and man of letters, depicts only square houses, which may only have been an artistic convention of his.)

Some structures in the new Tunica settlement must have been built by the Houma, which could explain the inconsistency in architectural styles. Charlevoix observed that the home of the Tunica chief, Cahura-Joligo, was square. This may indicate that the square houses were of Houma origin, because this structure probably was originally the Houma's temple. Years earlier Gravier had described the temple of the Houma as having

> a vestibule which is adorned with the most agreeable grotesques and the best made almost that one could see. They are four satyrs . . . standing out from the wall, having around the head, hands and feet in bands, bracelets, garters, [ornamented] belts, snakes, mice and dogs. The colors are black, white, red and yellow, and so well applied and without confusion, that it is a spectacle that surprises agreeably.

In 1721, Charlevoix seemed to note these same features in his description of the Tunica chief's house, which he called "quite ornamented for the house of a savage, with figures in relief that are not as bad as you might expect." If the two structures were indeed the same, Cahura-Joligo possibly had moved into the Houma temple in order to signify the Tunica's domination of their new land.

During this period it appears that the Tunica essentially maintained their traditional religious beliefs. Although Jean-Baptiste Bénard de la Harpe, a French explorer who encountered the Tunica in 1719, felt that they had abandoned the "greater part of their idolatry," he noted that they still kept the sacred images of a frog and a woman. The tribe's burial customs remained fundamentally unchanged. Archaeologists have found very few Christian emblems in Tunica graves of this period, which suggests that missionaries' teachings had little immediate impact.

By 1710, Father Davion had abandoned his permanent mission among the Tunica, although he returned to visit many times during the subsequent decade. His attempts to convert the tribe to Christianity had essentially failed. He had baptized some children and some dying adults, but these people had had little say in the matter. Davion's most notable success was his baptism of Cahura-Joligo, but Father Paul du Poisson, who visited the Tunica in 1727, considered the chief a Christian in name only. Charlevoix recorded in 1721 that the Tunica had no temple, a lack he attributed to the Indians' supposed religious apathy rather than to

Davion's influence. However, a sketch of the Tunica village made only a few years later by François Dumont de Montigny depicts a temple as the focus of village life. Moreover, at about this same time Father Poisson made remarks that indicate that the Tunica temple fire was still burning. But even though the Tunica apparently retained their traditional religion, Davion had sown some seeds of Christian faith that would eventually bear fruit.

Although Davion had stopped visiting Tunica territory in 1720, the French sustained a continual presence there. The visitors of record can have been only a tiny fraction of the explorers, colonists, soldiers, traders, and

Jean-Baptiste Bénard de la Harpe, a French explorer and observer of Tunica society in the early 1700s.

others who came to stay among the tribe at this time. There is even some evidence that a permanent French settlement was established in its territory. As early as 1712, a few French "strag-glers" lived among the Tunica. By 1722, there were 21 French men, women, and children. The following year, Bernard Diron d'Artaguiette, Inspector General of Louisiana, noted the presence of 15

Archaeologists excavating an 18th-century Tunica grave in the 1970s. The artifacts unearthed at such digs helped the Tunica prove the continuity of their culture and thus obtain recognition by the U.S. government in 1981.

Father Pierre François Xavier de Charlevoix, who visited the Tunica in the 1720s.

French "places"—probably meaning households—in the Tunica's homeland. By 1726, the 15 families comprised 48 people, a considerable French presence that was confirmed by Father Poisson in 1727.

François Dumont de Montigny's sketch of the Tunica village from this period shows both French houses and a temporary fort, named Loubois, near the tribe. French maps from the early 1700s also place several colonial habitations close to the Portage de la Croix. Although these settlements never grew to the size of the French communities among many other tribes, they were large enough to keep the Tunica firmly committed to the French cause. The tribe in turn benefited from the relative abundance of European goods it was able to attain from the nearby French.

The Tunica's prosperity during this period was due in large part to the leadership of their strong but accommodating chief, Cahura-Joligo. He solidly allied his tribe to the French and personally even adopted European clothing and learned some of the French language. The French bestowed medals and titles on him and relied on his military assistance. Although the Tunica officially recognized two chiefs, one for war and another for civil affairs, Cahura-Joligo often assumed both roles. His greatest role, however, was economic.

Charlevoix noted in 1721 that Cahura-Joligo "understands his trade very well. He has learned [from] us to hoard up money, and he is reckoned very rich." Under his leadership, the Tunica became prominent as suppliers of horses, fowl, corn, salt, and other products to the French. They were still only minor participants in the intercolonial deerskin trade, however. In 1726, Jean-Baptiste Le Moyne, sieur de Bienville, the governor of French Louisiana and founder of New Orleans, noted that "only one thousand deerskins can be obtained from them." But the Tunica supplied the basic needs of the colony remarkably well.

The tribe's accumulation of European goods was not achieved through trade alone. As consistent allies of France, the Tunica received annual presents as well as other gifts. The French gave them to the tribe even though the Tunica's lack of military strength limited their ability to help their French allies battle their enemies. Bienville estimated, for example, that the tribe could muster only 120 warriors in 1726.

Tunica warriors did take part in French military ventures and were well rewarded for their efforts. In 1712, for example, a Tunica contingent accompanied a French expedition up the Red River to establish a post, which was later named Natchitoches after a tribe living there. But despite the Tunica's occasional military support, the French did not always trust their warriors completely. The leader of one French expedition chose to build his encampment in a defensible position some distance away from his supposed allies.

Eventually, Tunica military assistance was directed largely against the Natchez Indians, on whose territory the French had established Fort Rosalie in 1716. The colonists had troubled and increasingly hostile relations with this tribe. In 1715 and 1716, the Tunica helped the French in their first war against the Natchez. As a reward for his tribe's aid, Cahura-Joligo received a commission as brigadier of the Red Armies, a largely honorary title, which bestowed little if any additional power on the chief.

In 1723, the Tunica again demonstrated their loyalty to the French by killing three Natchez warriors, even though the Tunica were allied with the Natchez at the time. Later that same year they joined a second French campaign against this tribe, during which Cahura-Joligo was badly wounded. As the Natchez prepared for their final showdown with the French, they did not even consider including the Tunica in their war plans, because they thought the tribe was "too much wedded to the French," according to Antoine Simon Le Page du Pratz, a colonist and memoirist.

After conspiring with the Yazoo and Chickasaw tribes, Natchez warriors launched a surprise attack on Fort Rosalie on November 29, 1729. The Indians killed or captured all but 20 of the 700 French men, women, and children at the surrounding colony. Also among the dead was a contingent of six Tunica warriors. A month later, the Yazoo Indians decimated another French garrison at Fort St. Pierre at the mouth of the Yazoo River. In only a few weeks, the substantial French presence in the region had been forever destroyed.

France could not afford to allow such acts to go unpunished. In 1730, a force of French troops descended on the Natchez and drove them from their villages, but most of the Indians escaped unharmed. Some Tunica joined the French army in the first attack, but apparently the tribe was not involved in the final French expedition against the Natchez the next year. During that battle, most of the Natchez were killed or enslaved, and the tribe essentially ceased to exist. Thereafter, only a few French soldiers were assigned to the region, because France lacked the willpower and the resources to revive settlement there. The Tunica would soon suffer the consequences of the French withdrawal.

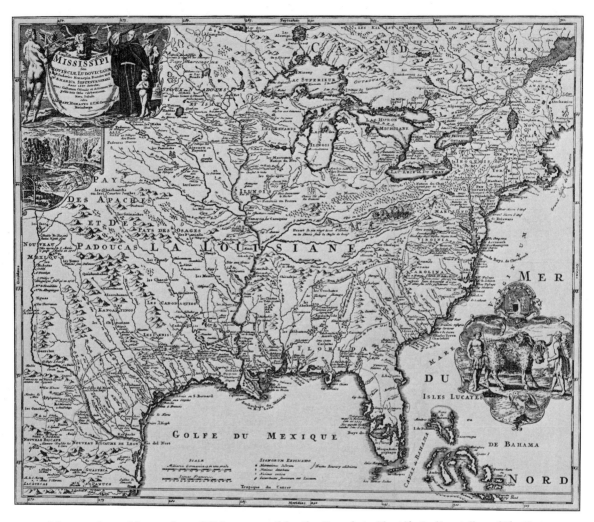

Maps such as this one from 1718 were used by the French to identify Indian tribes. (The Tunica are labeled here as the Tonikas.) They also helped the French substantiate the extent of their colonial rule.

In June 1731, misjudging the resentment of the Natchez, Cahura-Joligo welcomed a band of the tribe's survivors into his village. His act would result in the greatest disaster in recorded Tunica history.

One may wonder why a great chief who had so successfully guided his nation through many conflicts would have made such a misguided decision. Perhaps he recalled past friendly relations with the Natchez. Perhaps he felt

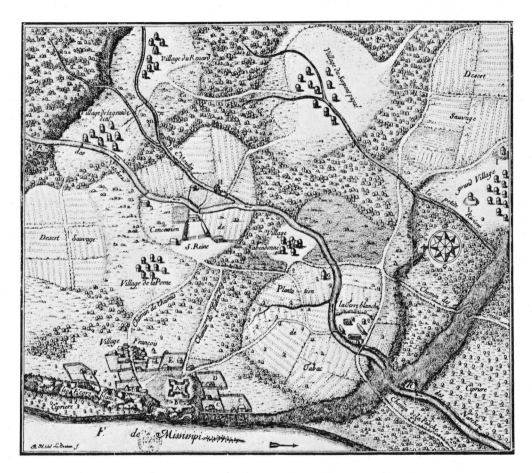

A diagram of Fort Rosalie and vicinity (present-day Natchez, Mississippi) in 1728. The following year, Natchez Indians destroyed the French outpost.

that the relative insignificance of the Tunica's role in the destruction of the Natchez was more than offset by the Natchez's murder of the six Tunica warriors in the 1729 Fort Rosalie massacre. Maybe Cahura-Joligo was just getting old. According to historical records, he had been chief for at least 15 years. Possibly he was the leader who had brought his people from the lower Yazoo River region 25 years earlier.

The details of what happened that June night are sketchy. There was a feast and a dance. Then, in the early morning hours, after the Tunica had retired, the Natchez attacked their hosts. They took possession of the village and assassinated Cahura-Joligo, although not before he killed several Natchez. The Tunica war chief rallied his warriors, and after a few days of battle, the Tunica regained the village and forced their treacherous guests out of the vicinity. On each side, at least 20 people were killed and as many wounded and captured. This loss cut the already small Tunica fighting force in half. Their leader was dead, and their village was destroyed, along with their food supply, munitions, and arms—essentially everything they had been given by their French friends. Under the circumstances, the Tunica decided once again to leave their home and settle elsewhere.

After three decades of contact with the French, the Tunica had moved from the fringes of colonial influence to its core. They had integrated economically and militarily with the new settlers. Many Tunica had become at least nominally Christian; children were often baptized, and a few women observed the rites of the Catholic church. Most adult males, however, resisted adopting the Europeans' religion, saying (in the words of Bénard de la Harpe) "the rules were too hard"—meaning they were not about to give up having more than one wife. (Yet some Tunica men did enjoy ringing the church bell before services.)

The Tunica had avidly accepted European goods and weapons, yet they continued to make many of their traditional objects, such as shell ornaments and pottery. They had adopted new ways while preserving many of their ancestral customs. This adaptability would serve them well in the coming struggle among the French, English, and Spanish for possession of the Mississippi River valley. ▲

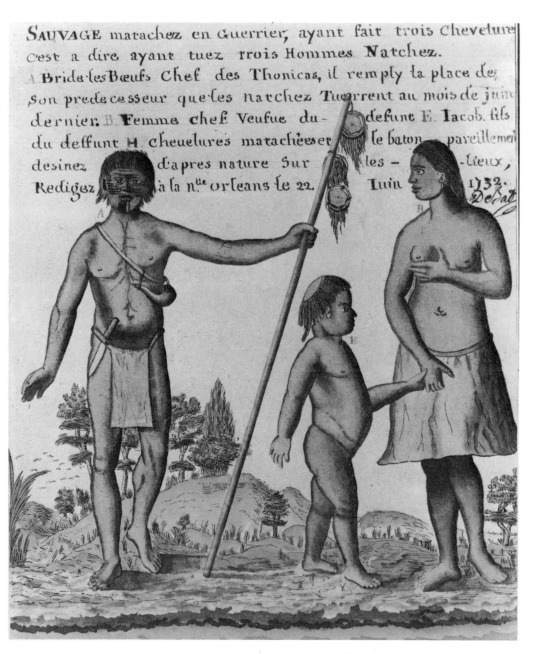

An 18th-century Tunica man, child, and woman. The inscription on this 1732 watercolor by Alexandre De Batz identifies the figure to the left as Bride-les-Boeufs (Buffalo Tamer), an important Tunica chief.

TUNICA BAYOU

In 1731, the Tunica relocated only a few miles south of Portage de la Croix on the banks of a bayou that still bears the tribe's name. The new site brought them even closer to their French friends, on whom they came to depend more than ever. It also left them in easy reach of old Indian trading partners along the Mississippi and Red rivers.

Greatly reduced in numbers after the Natchez's 1731 attack, the Tunica now gathered into a single village. (The village was excavated in the 1970s; the area is now known as the Trudeau site, after a French landowner who held the property briefly.) There the Tunica grouped their houses around a central plaza, as they had done in the past. The village also included part of a bluff that was naturally formed into the shape of the mounds the Tunica had once built in their previous homelands. The bluff was apparently used for the same pur-poses as their mounds. A structure was constructed on the bluff's summit. Some of the artifacts discovered there from this period are of a type found nowhere else—rare and treasured objects, such as pottery and wineglasses, that demonstrate both the tribe's trade activities and craft skills.

The Trudeau site was to become the source of the "Tunica Treasure," the most extraordinary collection of Indian and European artifacts from the colonial period ever excavated in the lower Mississippi Valley. The presence of the artifacts at the Tunica's village indicates that the tribe was quickly able to obtain replacements for the European goods it had lost at the hands of the Natchez. They probably could accumulate so many European-made objects because they were one of the few tribes left in the region with a significant and organized population. The French therefore still found them to be useful economic and military allies, even though their numbers had been reduced to, at most, only several hundred people. Their military importance to the French receives particular emphasis in the records of the period.

Tunica culture was changing as the people continued to adopt elements of the French way of life. Acculturation was never forced on the Tunica, however. Just as when they had been led by Cahura-Joligo, they seemed to want to accommodate the French. Although there was occasional friction between the French and the Tunica, the two groups never had a serious confrontation. Each needed the other. The result of that interdependence in the mid-1700s was an era of Tunica prosperity.

During this period, however, the Tunica maintained a regard for their own artifacts, working methods, and beliefs. Although they were influenced by the French and their goods, they remained a people—one in transition, to be sure, but also one with much of its own culture intact.

The artifacts of the Tunica Treasure were removed from graves located within the tribe's village compound. The graves tell us much about tribal life in the middle of the 18th century. Their contents included more European articles than the tribe had had before, but they were placed in the graves according to the Tunica's traditional burial arrangement—with weapons by the body's side and pottery by the head. Also in the graves were traditional Indian objects, such as shell ornaments and some stone tools. This indicates that the Tunica continued to manufacture these items after their move to the Tunica Bayou.

If such remnants were only found in graves, we could not be certain that the objects were actually used in the

Several items from the "Tunica Treasure," an extensive collection of objects dating from the mid-18th century that were excavated at Tunica Bayou in the 1970s. The pieces had been buried in graves as religious offerings.

Tunica's daily life; they might have been buried with the dead only because they had symbolic value. But such artifacts have also been unearthed in Tunica *middens* (refuse heaps). One large refuse pit found by archaeologists contained a vast array of items that corresponded to those found in the graves. Moreover, many metal artifacts were still usable, and some broken items that had been discarded might have been repaired. Clearly, the Tunica of this time could afford to be as free—perhaps even wasteful—with their goods in life as in death.

The same refuse pit gives further evidence of the Tunica's prosperity. Prominent in the remains are bones of bears, buffalo, and deer. The nearby uplands (called the Tunica Hills) and the lowlands across the Mississippi were rich hunting grounds, and the small tribal population could obviously afford to be selective in its diet. The Tunica also ate domesticated chickens and occasionally wild birds and fish. They grew corn, squash, and pumpkins and gathered wild fruits, nuts, and vegetables as well.

The Tunica also drank well—perhaps too well. The large number of bottles and other drink containers found at the Trudeau site indicates that they had steady access to alcoholic spirits. Indeed, in 1758, the governor of Louisiana, Louis Billouart, Chevalier de Kerlerec, specifically attributed the decline of the Tunica population to "the drink that has been so liberally lavished upon them for more than twenty years."

A kettle unearthed from the Tunica Bayou site. The presence of many such objects, still in serviceable condition, testifies to the prosperity of the tribe during their years there.

The tribe was not only well fed but relatively secure economically and politically. The Tunica's political structure seems to have reverted to its traditional division of power between a civil chief and a war chief after the death of Cahura-Joligo, because in the records of this period many chiefs are mentioned. In artist Alexandre De Batz's caption to his 1732 watercolor of a Tunica man named Bride-les-Boeufs (Buffalo Tamer), he refers to his subject as the chief of the Tunica, stating that "he took the place of his predecessor, whom the Natchez killed last June." In the previous year, observers had mentioned

A Tunica temple, drawn by Alexandre De Batz in 1732. Under French rule, the Tunica slowly incorporated Catholic beliefs into their traditional religion.

Bride-les-Boeufs as being only one of several eminent Tunica men. He was probably a war chief, and perhaps DeBatz simply meant to single him out as the one who had rallied the Tunica after Cahura-Joligo's murder. Nonetheless, Bride-les-Boeufs seems to have remained influential for the next 30 years and was still spoken of as a chief in 1764.

Two other men of distinction, Lattanash and Carodet, are also mentioned as chiefs later in this period. In fact, Lattanash, who outlived Bride-les-Boeufs, was recognized as principal chief as late as 1771. During the mid-1700s one chief may have been recognized as preeminent, but it appears that his power was nonetheless shared.

Although the remains of the Tunica's temple and burial sites indicate that they still maintained their traditional beliefs, the Indians' religious practices are not discussed in historical documents of the period. The only outright references to religion indicate that the tribe also continued to observe some hallmarks of Christianity. Many Tunica used their baptismal names, and when those who had known Father Davion as children reached adulthood, they in turn had their own offspring christened. In 1740 alone, 27 Tunica children were baptized by the "consent and demand" of their parents. Among the parents was Chief Carodet, who was also known by his Christian name, Jean Louis. In the Tunica Treasure, however, there are only four crucifixes and a handful of rosary beads. Most likely the veneer of Christianity overlay and mingled with the continuance of traditional religious practice. Demonstrations of having been converted to Christianity probably also helped the Tunica deal with the French, who were a growing presence in their midst.

Although the tribe remained economically significant to Louisiana during the period, its real importance was military. The few survivors of the Natchez people mounted guerrilla attacks on French settlements well into the 1740s and remained a threat for years thereafter. Many Natchez survivors found refuge among the pro-English Chickasaw tribe to the northeast. Despite the demands of the French, the Chickasaw refused to stop harboring Natchez refugees. This helped bring about another series of confrontations, known as the Chickasaw Wars, during the 1730s. The wars proved disastrous for the French in Louisiana. They were enormously costly, but worse, they caused the French to lose the support of some of their Indian allies and, consequently, their credibility as a military power in the eyes of European rivals. Ultimately, this would severely limit

their control of the lower Mississippi Valley.

The Tunica helped the French counter Natchez incursions both in and around their ancestral home. The French apparently rewarded them considerably for these and other services. The Tunica essentially became a paid native auxiliary to the French colonial military.

Tunica warriors served the French in many skirmishes from the 1730s through the 1750s. Successive governors of the Louisiana colony recognized their debt to the tribe. In 1733, Etienne de Perier called the Tunica "the best nation, although small, that the king has in his service." In 1751, Pierre Ri-

Two crucifixes found in graves at Tunica Bayou.

gaud, Marquis de Vaudreuil, expressed satisfaction with "the Indians, with whom we have reason to be pleased." And Kerlerec noted in 1758 that though possessing only about 60 warriors, "this nation . . . is very brave and has always served the French well."

Curiously, however, there is little archaeological evidence from the period of the Tunica's military involvement. No trophies and remarkably few firearms have been found at the Trudeau site, even though it is unlikely that firearms were in short supply. Although the Tunica acted as subordinates of the French, their perception of themselves was possibly somewhat different.

Two incidents of the period seem to indicate that the tribe was not just a reflexive French ally. It instead possessed certain priorities of its own that probably justified the nagging French suspicion that *les sauvages* (the savages), as the French called all Indians, could not be fully trusted. In 1736, the Tunica were implicated in an attempt by the Chakchiuma Indians to establish a peace (and by implication an economic relationship) with the Chickasaw and the English. The Tunica's role in this plan was to induce the tribes along the Red River, such as the Avoyel and Natchitoches, to join in the alliance. Apparently, the head Tunica chief and several other leaders entered into this "chimerical project," as the Louisiana governor later called it. Bienville, however, managed to bribe two Tunica war chiefs while the head chief was away on his Red River mission. On his return, the head chief was made to see his folly, and the Tunica resumed their pro-French stance. They demonstrated their renewed loyalty by attacking the Chakchiuma and looting and burning their village, which happened to be located on the former Tunica homeland on the Yazoo River. In the process, the Tunica gained a great deal of booty.

Jean-Baptiste Le Moyne, sieur de Bienville, founder of New Orleans and colonial governor of Louisiana for several terms. Bienville praised the Tunica as a "brave nation" that had given the French "proof of its devotion."

Indians overrunning a British stronghold during the French and Indian War. The British victory in 1763 led the Tunica to relocate in order to stay near their French allies.

In 1737, a second incident illustrated the tribe's growing differences with the French. "Several riotous [Tunica] men" murdered a Frenchman, according to Bienville. The French retaliated for the alcohol-induced slaying, and heads rolled—at least one and perhaps two. They were said to have been the heads of Tunica chiefs.

Two years following this, a French officer recorded in his journal that the Tunica had "much degenerated in the qualities which they had originally possessed for war." It was certainly true that their numbers had declined. But they continued to make a substantial contribution to French enterprises in the region. In truth, it was the French themselves who were suffering the greater loss of military power.

By the mid-1700s, there began a series of conflicts today called the French and Indian War (1754–63). This struggle pitted the French and the English

RELOCATIONS OF THE TUNICA, 1541–1800

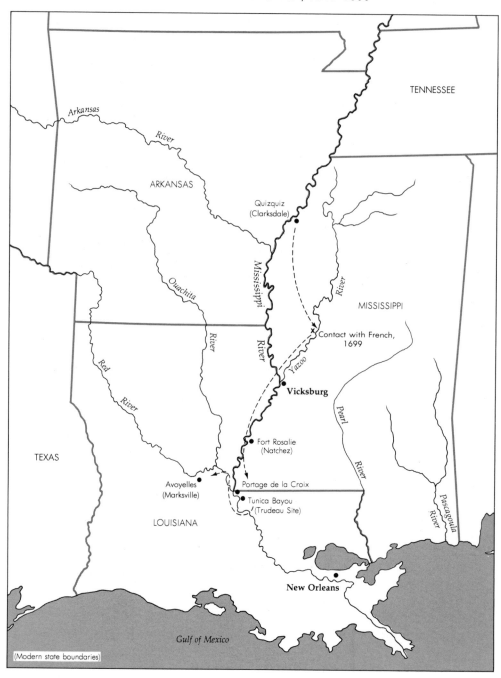

TENNESSEE

Arkansas

River

ARKANSAS

Quizquiz
(Clarksdale)

Ouachita

Mississippi

River

River

Yazoo

MISSISSIPPI

River

× Contact with French,
1699

Red

River

● **Vicksburg**

TEXAS

Pearl

● Fort Rosalie
(Natchez)

River

Avoyelles ●
(Marksville)

Portage de la Croix

Pascagoula

● Tunica Bayou
(Trudeau Site)

River

LOUISIANA

New Orleans

Gulf of Mexico

(Modern state boundaries)

against each other for control of eastern North America. During this time, the two countries were at war on their home ground of Europe as well.

In 1761, Spain joined in the conflict on the side of France. Spain had been a bitter rival of England for centuries and felt loyalty toward France because the monarchs of the two countries were related. In appreciation for the alliance, France ceded its land west of the Mississippi River to Spain in 1762 under provisions of the Treaty of Fontainebleau. Louisiana consequently came under Spanish control, although it retained its French character.

But despite the Spanish-French alliance, Britain won the wars in both Europe and North America. With the signing of the Treaty of Paris, which concluded the French and Indian War, France in 1763 ceded all its land east of the Mississippi to England. Spain surrended to Britain its claims to Florida.

During these conflicts the Tunica had, naturally, allied themselves with the French. They would subsequently become the allies of the Spanish as the latter took control over Louisiana. As a result, hostility grew between the Tunica and the English with their Indian allies.

In March 1764, the Tunica and some other Indians ambushed the first English convoy to attempt an ascent of the Mississippi after the 1763 Treaty of Paris had given the English the right to navigate the river. The attack forced the convoy to return downriver. The English, of course, blamed the French, and the defeated French in turn officially berated the Tunica for not welcoming the newcomers.

It is doubtful that the Tunica and their friends had acted on their own initiative, however. They had policed the Mississippi for the French for decades. Their act was probably one last unofficial—but tacitly sanctioned—display of bravado. The Tunica no doubt relished the excursion. They had suffered greatly at the hands of the English and their Indian allies, and they surely feared what the coming English presence might bring in the future.

The Tunica publicly justified the attack by saying that they did not wish to give up a slave who had fled from the English to their protection. They added, according to a French colonial administrator, that the English had "bad hearts" and had "corrupted the ways among all the tribes." Nonetheless, at the prompting of French officals they contritely apologized to the English. Despite strong protests from the soldiers they had humiliated, they escaped punishment. It was on this unpromising note that the Tunica came, briefly, under English rule. ▲

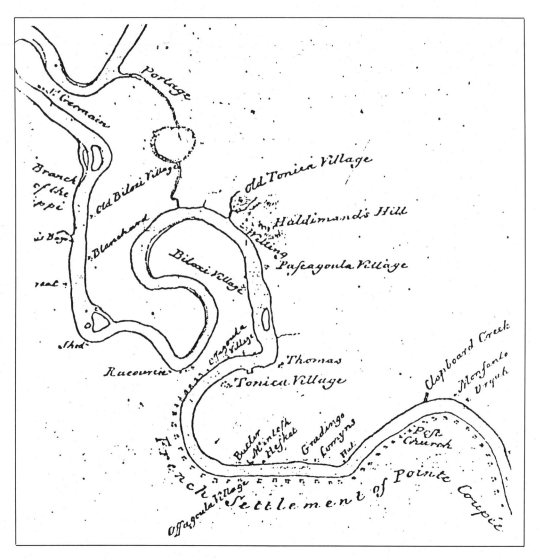

The vicinity of Pointe Coupée, drawn in 1770 by British surveyor George Gauld. By this time, the Tunica and the Biloxi had moved from their "old" villages, as labeled here, to ones closer to the French settlement.

SHIFTING ALLIANCES

After making their peace with the English in 1764, the Tunica settled on the east bank of the Mississippi River, about 15 miles south of Trudeau and at the northern edge of the French settlement of Pointe Coupee. Thus, though technically under English rule, they lived as close as possible to their long-time French allies and still preserved their tribal integrity. In this location, they could also continue to benefit from the river that was so vital to their existence. The Tunica would dwell at Pointe Coupee for the next 25 years.

This would be a time of great political change in the region, as events happening elsewhere in North America began to affect all the people who lived along the banks of the Mississippi. During the 1770s, while Spain assumed administrative control of Louisiana, England lost control of its own North American colonies as its subjects there declared independence. Spain joined in the American Revolution (1776–83) on the side of the colonists. It sought not so much to help the revolutionaries as to protect its investment in Louisiana and damage the hated English. Under Bernardo de Galvez, the new governor of Louisiana, Spanish forces in 1781 formally took back the much-contested area south of the 13 colonies and east of the Mississippi known as West Florida. Thus, within a 20-year period, the Tunica at Pointe Coupee experienced first English and then Spanish rule.

Unfortunately, the Pointe Coupee village site has been destroyed by meanderings of the Mississippi River, so that no archaeological evidence remains of the Tunica's occupation of the area. There is also a scarcity of historical information for this period in the lower Mississippi Valley because of the region's volatile political situation.

The English never quite achieved a secure grasp of West Florida. Having fought the French for nearly a century to gain control of the Mississippi, they found their foothold on it in the 1760s frustrated by the Spanish, whose possession of New Orleans gave them control over the river's outlet to the sea. Distracted by discontent growing among their colonies on the Atlantic Coast, the English from the outset were unable to realize the potential of their new dominion.

Spanish rule is also poorly documented. Spain had been reluctant to assume possession of Louisiana. It viewed this vast new territory mostly as a buffer for its colonies in the Caribbean and Mexico. The Spanish government in Louisiana was never more than an administrative veneer over the French culture already established there.

Finally, although there was a flood of American settlers to the region during this period, they did not have the scholarly or religious interest in the Indians there that French visitors in the 18th century had shown. (Indeed, most were barely literate if they could read at all.) Therefore, few of the settlers left behind written records. Nonetheless, a few facts about the Tunica survive, from which we may make some surmises about their life during these years.

The Tunica village at Pointe Coupee was estimated by several British visitors to consist of about 30 huts in 1766, though by the end of the English administration it was apparently somewhat smaller. A map drawn in 1770 depicts two rows of at least a dozen houses each. If it is accurate, it indicates a significant change from the Tunica's tradition of grouping their houses in a circle. The map also seems to depict a large community-owned cornfield near the village. Additional documentation from British administrators records a peach orchard and separate camps of hunters.

By this time hunting had become the Tunica's major means of obtaining food, and game animals were their principal contribution to colonial trade. Jean Jacques Blaise d'Abbadie, Louisiana governor during the transition from French to Spanish rule, wrote, "It is not possible for us to do away entirely with powder and ball as gifts to the savages, who no longer make their living except by hunting with the gun, and contribute by that means to our own subsistence and to a part of the commerce of this colony." Tunica hunters were sometimes hired by non-Indians. French naval officer Jean-Bernard Bossu wrote that during his 1771 journey up the Mississippi he was "obliged to hire two savages of the Tonikas nation to hunt during the course of our trip. They obtained for us an abundance of food while we were going up the river." One Tunica on the expedition displayed his marksmanship by shooting a rattlesnake that was swimming across the river. For this feat he was honored with the title Chevalier of the Rattlesnake, and the figure of a serpent was tattooed around his body.

The Tunica of Pointe Coupee had become a semiacculturated people. They still tattooed themselves, but they also often wore articles of European clothing. Leaders owned complete suits, which they donned at least on public occasions. (However, Bossu observed that one of the leaders would wear every part of his suit but his pants.)

The Tunica continued to have their children baptized, but there is no evidence that their involvement with the church extended much beyond this. They conducted themselves with sophisticated decorum in the day-to-day colonial affairs of state. Yet Lieutenant John Thomas, the English Indian agent (an official charged by his government with dealing with the Indians), noted that on at least one occasion they still performed the "barbarous and ancient exhibitions of the Indians, cutting themselves with the teeth or bones of fish till the blood ran in streams, to show their warlike disposition."

Despite such displays, Governor d'Abaddie contrasted the Tunica's gentleness with the drunken behavior of the Pacana, a briefly neighboring tribe that was in transit from Mobile. The Tunica themselves were not immune to alcohol abuse, however, and observers continued to note their immoderate use of liquor. It was a peril that native medicine could not treat, al-

Bernardo de Galvez, who became Spain's governor over colonial Louisiana in 1777. In the Tunica's last recorded military venture, tribal warriors helped de Galvez and his men capture Baton Rouge from the British in 1779.

though one Tunica medicine man was famous for his cure by herbs and other natural formulas of lesser ills, such as rheumatism, gout, and kidney stones. Tunica medicine men also acted as spiritual counselors, casting spells and exorcising demons, and used their prestige to influence tribal decisions.

The principal chief during this time was the aged Lattanash. Initially, he ap-

A trigger mechanism—all that remains of a rifle excavated from a Tunica site. By the late 1700s, hunting had become as important as trade to the tribe's survival.

parently shared power with others. In 1764, Bride-les-Boeufs and Perruquier (Wigmaker) were mentioned as important lesser chiefs. Bride-les-Boeufs, although also elderly by this time, probably continued in the position of war chief. Perruquier, who was an Ofo Indian, was a spokesman for the remnants of that tribe, which joined the Tunica during this decade.

The economic and military importance of the Tunica was much reduced by their declining numbers, but they remained the leading Indian nation in the region. The English and Spanish vied for their loyalty with presents. They bestowed medals, flags, and other regalia upon the chiefs. The tribe accepted gifts from both sides, generally without suffering for it, thus demonstrating their ability to survive under tense circumstances. In fact, they apparently did quite well in their negotiations with both parties, although the Spanish were more generous than their English competitors.

In 1769, the value of the annual Spanish gift to the Tunica was more than 121 pesos, a sum greater than that given to any other tribe in this part of the Mississippi Valley. In 1772, the English agent John Thomas complained to his superior that the presents at his disposal "amounted to less for all the tribes [in the river valley] than the Spanish provided for the Tonicas alone." Thomas sniffed that the Tunica and their neighbors were simply "importunate beggars." Not wishing to lose the Indians' allegiance, however, the English increased the number of their gifts enough to induce the Tunica to remain on the Mississippi's east bank.

The rivalry between the English and the Spanish for Indian loyalty was more a matter of national pride than military necessity. Although both sides had hoped initially to enlist Indian allies to guard their respective riverbank borders, such plans were soon cast aside. The tribes were simply too small, weak, and indifferent for the purpose. Yet the

Tunica had demonstrated their warlike disposition during their 1764 attack on the first English convoy on the Mississippi. Tunica warriors were probably also among the 160 Indians who helped Governor de Galvez and his Spanish army capture the British-held town of Baton Rouge in 1779. This was the last recorded military venture of the Tunica.

The Tunica were content under Spanish rule. Their temporary, dubious allegiance to the English had been a political necessity, but even then they had demonstrated a penchant for their French and Spanish neighbors west of the Mississippi. Once both banks came under the flag of Spain, the Tunica were relieved of the delicate business of diplomacy. In November 1779, having gained complete control of the land along the Mississippi, Galvez ordered "all officers and soldiers and inhabitants under His Catholic Majesty to respect and protect the rights of the tribe of Thonicas." It was a sincere attempt to protect Indians in their holdings. Christianized Indians—as the Tunica were now officially considered to be— even had the same legal right to land as white settlers.

Eastern non-Indian settlers, who had been encouraged to immigrate by both the English and Spanish governments, soon began to flood the region, however. The influx so irritated the Tunica that they decided to abandon their Pointe Coupee village. Sometime in the late 1780s or early 1790s, they relocated to a site along the Red River near what is now Marksville, Louisiana,

An Indian peace medal with a bust of King George III of Britain. The English conferred such medals on Tunica chiefs in a failed attempt to gain the tribe's loyalty.

where they had been granted land by the Spanish governor. Other small tribes in the area, such as the Ofo, Biloxi, and Avoyel, were, like the Tunica, seeking to preserve their Indian heritage. Soon these peoples would be inextricably linked with their Tunica neighbors.

The Tunica had learned to adapt to several colonial cultures during the late 18th century. Soon after their final migration, the beneficent Spanish rule would be replaced by that of the expanding United States. This change would test the tribe's adaptability and move the Tunica people toward even greater acculturation. ▲

Detail from Louisiana Indians Walking Along a Bayou, *painted in 1847 by Alfred Boisseau. The boy holds darts and a blowgun, a weapon the Tunica took up in the 1800s to hunt birds and small game.*

A

FORGOTTEN
PEOPLE

The Tunica's choice of present-day Marksville, Louisiana, for their new home was a logical one. Having left the banks of the Mississippi to avoid the influx of non-Indian homesteaders from the East, the tribe now decided to live along the Red River—another great avenue of trade, but one that opened to the west. Marksville, then known as Avoyelles after the Avoyel Indians, stood on an elevated plain that overlooked the level lands along the Red River—an area that was figuratively known as Prairie Island. The prairie was the first large habitable area one encountered while traveling up the Red River away from its junction with the Mississippi. Thus, the prairie's inhabitants could easily control access to the larger river. Once again the Tunica had purposely chosen a strategic location.

Over the course of the 1800s, railroads would gradually supersede riverways as Americans' preferred mode of trade, transportion, and communication, and the strategic value of the Tunica's new home would diminish accordingly. But the location also offered good farmland, abundant wildlife, natural foodstuffs, and good fishing. Indeed, the locale has remained so inviting that the Tunica still live there today.

The 19th century was a time of enormous change for the United States as a whole. Although the Marksville area was generally a quiet backwater, the change was felt there and noticeably transformed the Tunica way of life.

The U.S. government acquired Louisiana in 1803 as a result of a series of events that occurred in Europe. Beginning in 1789, a revolution had shaken France and destroyed its monarchy. Napoleon Bonaparte rapidly rose to power during the resulting chaos.

Spain, embroiled in the European wars that followed, neglected its various colonies in the Americas. Ultimately, Napoleon forced Spain to sign a secret agreement, the Treaty of Ildefonso, in which it returned Louisiana to France. Napoleon had visions of a French empire in North America but found himself short of the troops necessary to defend the territory. In need of funds with which to continue his European exploits, he sold the entire vast territory to the United States by treaty in 1803.

This milestone event, called the Louisiana Purchase, led to a flurry of U.S. surveys, reports, and head counts of the region's native inhabitants. But attention soon focused on the largely unknown and potentially hostile Indians who roamed the Great Plains. Many small and peaceable tribes in the South were virtually forgotten. Such was the fate of the Tunica, and it would prove a mixed blessing for the tribe.

The only U.S. government record of the Tunica between 1803 and 1938 was written in 1806 by John Sibley, federal Indian commissioner for Louisiana:

> These people formerly lived on the Bayou Tunica, above Pointe Coupee, on the Mississippi, East Side, live now at Avoyelles [Marksville]; do not, at present, exceed twenty-five men. Their native language is peculiar to themselves, but [they also] speak Mobilian [an intertribal trade language]; are employed occasionally by the inhabitants as boatmen, &c.; in amity with all other people, and gradually diminishing in number.

Despite the account's brevity, it provides a basis for comprehending the Tunica of the early 19th century. Even though the Tunica relocated, their population seems to have remained quite stable. They continued to speak their own language and to survive peaceably by hiring themselves out for work to their non-Indian neighbors. Their traditional culture most likely remained relatively unchanged.

At about the same time as Sibley's report, a French traveler, C. C. Robin, encountered a group of Indians on the Black River, a tributary of the Red River. The details of Robin's account suggests that they were Tunica, although he did not state the name of the tribe.

What Robin visited was apparently a temporary camp. It consisted of about a dozen families, who slept in tiny oval huts thatched with the broad, fan-shaped leaves of the palmetto. They carried with them pots made of iron, copper, wood, and clay. Robin observed that the Indians manufactured their clay pottery themselves by kneading ground-up shells into the clay before they fired their pottery. This was obviously a people with a tradition of ceramic arts.

It was spring, and the men were away hunting deer and bear to get skins, tallow, and oil for barter at the local trading posts. Robin also indicated that these Indians brought chickens and dogs with them and that they were not farmers, although they did grow a little corn in temporary plots. The members of the group were probably tem-

THE TUNICA IN MARKSVILLE, EARLY 1800s

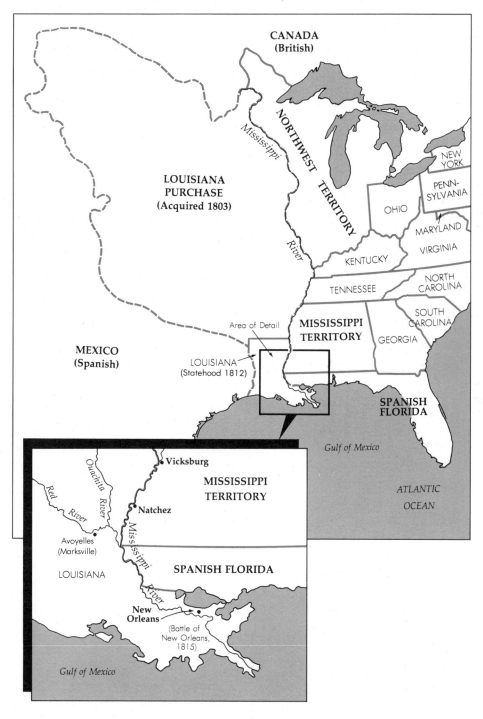

porarily excused from their agricultural duties because they were away from their homes on a hunting expedition.

The French traveler also noted the Indians' desire for liquor and ornaments and gives later in his narrative a perceptive account of the changes wrought by European contact on the Indian way of life:

With the arrival of firearms, far more efficient than arrows, it was possible for a single individual or at best a few hunters to engage in hunting. Thus every hunting affair ceased to be a public occasion, and the great celebrations became less frequent, and no longer involved the same ceremoniousness. The dances and games became obsolescent. Public affairs among the Indians deteriorated. They lived more in single families and small aggregations. They no longer needed to associate themselves into great nations except in time of war, against those who interfered with their hunting. War was thus almost the only bond left to them, but those peoples who were neighbors of the European settlers, no longer fearing destruction by enemy warriors, have almost ceased to exist as nations. They have gradually become dispersed in small bands and families,

Natchez, Mississippi, in the early 1800s. A U.S. government census in 1806 noted that Tunica were "employed occasionally by the [non-Indian] inhabitants as boatmen."

whose relationship to each other is only casual. At the same time, the use of firearms made them dependent upon the Europeans for guns, powder and lead, as well as for iron tools like hatchets and knives, which were far superior to those they had before. These they obtained in exchange for skins which they had formerly used as clothing, but now they accustomed themselves to replacing these with blankets and coarse cloth which were much more convenient. Thus, little by little, they got out of the habit of using skins as clothing.

In 1813, William Darby, a traveler and writer of guides for settlers, noted that "the Tonicas have adopted the manners and customs of the French. One or two white families reside amongst them, and it would puzzle Montesquieu [a famous French social observer] himself to determine which of the parties has been the most influenced by the other." Additionally, many tribes of the region became "Americanized" to a degree when their warriors joined a diverse group of homesteaders, backwoodsmen, free blacks, and militiamen under General Andrew Jackson to fight a common enemy: the British, whose persistent meddling in U.S. affairs had led to the War of 1812. In the war's final engagement, the 1815 Battle of New Orleans, Jackson's motley army resoundingly defeated the British and secured the United States's hold on the vast Louisiana Territory. There are no data, however, to show that Tunica were among

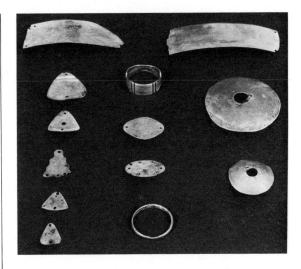

Nineteenth-century Tunica came to prefer metal ornaments such as these (sometimes called tinklers and janglers) to the shell beads they had used in years past.

the many Indian warriors in Jackson's party.

In an official view expressed in 1826, the Tunica remained "savages," because they were not using the land "as Providence had decided: for farming." The anonymous author of this report (from the federal registrar and recorder of the land office) apparently could not consider them "reclaimed from their savage mode of life" until they had "subdued their original propensities and evidenced a determination to live and cultivate the ground as white men do."

Historical documents and legal records indicate that the Tunica lived in a second village in addition to Marksville during the early years of the 19th century—apparently a settlement on

Bayou Rouge, a few miles to the south. Such a division between two permanent villages would explain references in documents of the time to the simultaneous existence of two Tunica chiefs; each village would have had its own headman. In any case, the tribe soon united at Marksville.

Although the following description, from the memoir of an escaped slave named Solomon Northrup, is of the Tunica's Chickasaw neighbors in the 1840s, it probably is an accurate account of the Tunica way of life as well during this time:

> They live in simple huts, 10 or 12 feet square, constructed of pine poles and covered with bark. They subsist principally on the flesh of deer, the coon, and opossum, all of which are plenty in these woods. Sometimes they exchange venison for a little corn and whisky with the planters on the bayous. Their usual dress is buckskin breeches and calico hunting shirts of fantastic colors, buttoned from belt to chin. They wear brass rings on their wrists, and in their ears and noses. The dress of the squaws is very similar. They are fond of dogs and horses—owning many of the latter, of a small, tough breed—and are skillful riders.

Tunica artifacts of the period reveal that the tribe was relatively prosperous. The objects are numerous, of high quality, and appear to be well used. Among them are guns, knives, and barbed fishing spears, from which we can infer that

hunting and fishing were important pursuits. The tribe now lived in an area where alligator- and turtle-hunting were fruitful pastimes. Hoes from this time indicate that the Tunica did not neglect their farming, official reports notwithstanding. Axes and large adzes—cutting tools used to shape wood—suggest that the Tunica practiced carpentry and heavy construction: Tunica houses at Marksville may have been as solidly built as those of their non-Indian neighbors. Stirrups and bridles reveal that they had horses. Their beadwork, paisley shirts, and silver ornaments show that they had learned to use non-Indian materials to make items with decidedly Indian, if not specifically Tunica, identity.

One category of artifacts is conspicuously absent: objects of distinctly Christian significance. This is surprising, for in the 18th century many Tunica had at least accepted some elements of the Catholic faith. The backwoods society of non-Indian Americans in the 1800s probably offered the Tunica more freedom to follow their traditional beliefs than had the French, and Tunica observance of their traditional burial customs endured through this era.

As the 19th century progressed, the Tunica's non-Indian neighbors would present the tribe with other problems. The Tunica's fundamental difficulty stemmed from homesteaders' insatiable desire for land. To accommodate the settlers, the federal government began to force large Indian tribes in the southeastern United States, such as the Cher-

Choctaw Village near the Chefuncte [River], *painted in 1869 by François Bernard. The houses, dress, and everyday objects and activities shown here are similar to those of the Tunica in the mid-1800s.*

okee of North Carolina and Georgia, to abandon their homelands en masse and relocate west of the Mississippi River. This policy was formally enacted by Congress in the Indian Removal Act of 1830. It was signed by Andrew Jackson, who had been elected president of the United States thanks in part to his popularity following his victory at the Battle of New Orleans. Jackson called the Indians an "unhappy, ill-fated race" and stated that removal would put them "beyond the reach of injury or oppression." The most immediate effect of his removal policy, however, was to free Indian-occupied land in the East for white settlement.

The Tunica were not removed to western lands, probably because their small population did not present a major obstacle to non-Indian settlers who wanted their lands. But the Tunica

(continued on page 84)

THE OTHER PEOPLES OF
THE TUNICA-BILOXI TRIBE

The Tunica-Biloxi tribe of Louisiana recognized today by the U.S. government is composed not only of the Tunica and Biloxi but also of the remnants of several other tribes from the lower Mississippi River valley. Among these peoples are the Mississippi Choctaw, Avoyel, and Ofo.

All these groups were descendants of the mound-building Mississippian people who had come to the area in about 1500 B.C. Because they had similar origins and shared the same environment, their societies had much in common prior to contact with Europeans. Many farmed the fertile lands along the Mississippi River and its tributaries. They also carried on a river-based trade with other tribes throughout the heartland of North America. The rivers and streams provided them with fish throughout the year, and they grew maize, pumpkins, beans, squash, and other agricultural products to round out their diet. A number also shared a sun-based religion.

Many of the peoples of the lower Mississippi Valley formed confederacies of city-states. The inhabitants of these were divided into classes of nobility and commoners. The Natchez, for example, dominated a confederacy that included the Yazoo, Taensa, and Avoyel Indians. Led by a ruler called the Great Sun, the confederacy classified its people as Suns, Nobles, Honored People, and the masses, who were also known as Stinkards.

These tribes even had similar pastimes. Like the Tunica, the Choctaw played a ball game similar to the modern sport of lacrosse. This game, which they called ishtaboli, was played by two teams of players, with each player holding two sticks made of hickory with a netted cup at one end. Players used these sticks to move a small rawhide ball down a playing field. Their object was to hit the ball into one of the two poles that were placed at opposite ends of the field. The winning team was the first to score a set number of goals, which varied from game to game.

The coming of European explorers and colonists to the lower Mississippi in the 17th and 18th centuries brought drastic change to the tribes in the region. From the outset, European diseases decimated their populations and weakened their ability to fend for themselves. Thereafter, these Indian groups faced the dilemma of how best to deal with the newcomers. Some chose to ally themselves with one European nation. For instance, the

Choctaw, like the Tunica, made an alliance with their new French neighbors. But other tribes chose outright hostility to all Europeans. The Natchez were especially belligerent and encountered unswerving antagonism in return. By the mid-1700s, they were destroyed as a people; the French had either killed or captured and sold into slavery almost the entire tribe. Smaller tribes, even several who had allied themselves to a European nation, suffered too; through attrition, many gradually ceased to exist.

The Biloxi, who traditionally lived along the coast of the Gulf of Mexico, were able to survive by relocating to avoid conflict with colonists. In 1702, only three years after their first contact with whites, they moved to Mobile

Tunica-Biloxi tribe members take part in the 1988 Corn Feast, along with representatives of the Caddo tribe. Many Indian peoples along the Mississippi celebrated a green corn festival, and their rites melded with those of the Tunica as they joined the tribe in Marksville.

Bay in present-day Alabama. By the 1760s they moved westward after this area passed from French to English control. Thereafter, their presence was recorded in various locations in present-day Mississippi, Louisiana, and Texas. In 1830, a doctor named Jean-Louis Berlandier, traveling on an expedition through Mexico and Texas, wrote:

> The Belocses, as the Spanish call them, or Biloxi in French, are a small nation. . . . For many years they lived along the Louisiana border, near the confluence of the Rigoles du Bon Dieu, where they had a few fields of maize and hunted in the forests. At that time they numbered about a hundred or so

An extended Houma family of the early 1900s. The Houma have always been downriver neighbors of the Tunica; in the 1700s the Tunica even seized one of their villages. Houma people continue to live along the Mississippi today, but the tribe is not officially recognized.

individuals, including a score or so of warriors. When France ceded Louisiana to the United States of North America, the Belocses moved into Texas territory, where they now dwell along the eastern bank of the Rio de Neches. Their numbers have not dwindled since then. There are still 25 families of them, with a hundred members at the very least.

Following the Louisiana Purchase of 1803, the United States government moved to establish control of Indian lands along the Mississippi. The Choctaw survived through the careful negotiation of treaties with the United States. They also began to assimilate into the dominant white culture. Many attended schools and Christian churches, and some even acquired black slaves. Within a few years, however, they were forced by the government to relocate to lands to the west. Most tribal members removed to Indian Territory (now Oklahoma) in the early 1830s.

Some, however, managed to stay on in Mississippi, where they soon found themselves surrounded by disdainful and often unscrupulous white settlers eager to seize their land. These Choctaw were also cut off from their own schools and churches, which had moved west with the majority of the tribe. Those who chose to remain in Mississippi had to struggle against great odds to maintain their group identity and traditional customs. (Nobel Prize–winning novelist William Faulkner, the great chronicler of the American South, was later to write of their struggle to endure in short stories such as "Red Leaves," "A Courtship," "Lo!" and "A Justice.")

Under the difficult circumstances of the 1800s some Mississippi Choctaw and the remnants of other ravaged tribes in the region, such as the Biloxi, began to integrate socially with and marry into the Tunica Indian community. Having relocated at the end of the 1700s to Avoyelles (now Marksville, Louisiana), where the Spanish had granted them refuge, the Tunica enjoyed enough stability and continuity to welcome these people. The resident Indians influenced the newcomers with their customs and beliefs and were influenced by them in turn. Variations in their already similar traditions and rituals, such as their annual green corn festivals, melded as the peoples intermingled. By the early 20th century, the cultures of these groups had been absorbed into the Tunica way of life. But although this fusion of peoples now functioned as a single tribe, years would pass before the community gained governmental recognition. Finally, after decades of legal struggle, the U.S. government in 1981 formally acknowledged the tribe under the joint name of the Tunica-Biloxi Indians of Louisiana.

A mid-19th century view of Vicksburg, Mississippi, site of a crucial Civil War battle. Warships seeking to protect or destroy Confederate supply routes navigated through the Tunica's homeland throughout the war.

(continued from page 79)
could not avoid such settlers. Few Indians at that time held legal deeds proving ownership of property, a situation that enabled conniving whites to force them out of their territory. One account relates that in 1841 the Tunica's chief, Melancon, pulled up fence posts planted by one such villain on tribal land. The culprit, who had been appointed head of an Indian patrol by his neighbors, shot Melancon in the head in view of several other tribal members. The killer never stood trial and succeeded in taking control of some of the Tunica's territory.

Subsequent litigations relating to the death of Melancon seem, not surprisingly, to have been traumatic events for the Tunica. The tribe received no justice from government officials, who still generally considered them "savages" undeserving of full legal rights. In many respects, this point in the 19th century marks a period of decline for the tribe, from which it is only now recovering.

Unfortunately, little information exists on the effect of the Civil War (1861–65) on the Tunica. However, their location, earlier so advantageous for trade, must have made life uncomfortable. The Mississippi and the Red rivers became watery battlegrounds as the Union tried to cut the Confederacy in half by gaining command of the shipping channels. Gunboats commanded by Union admiral David Farragut steamed the Mississippi from New Orleans to Vicksburg, working to establish a naval blockade of supplies; and in 1864, Union general Nathaniel Banks attempted an abortive expedition to gain control of the Red River, at the very center of Tunica life.

During these years, the Tunica apparently decided the best way to protect themselves was simply by keeping a low profile. After Melancon's death, the very existence of a Tunica chieftaincy became a tribal secret. Even so, the tribe's economic position became ever more precarious. Indians deprived of their land often fell into debt after they tried *sharecropping*—farming on land owned by another in exchange for a share of the money paid for the crop. The Tunica generally continued fishing, hunting, and farming—now more for their own subsistence than for money. They also raised cash crops of cotton, vegetables, and pecans, kept chickens, and performed work for wages. They were no longer prosperous, but they survived.

In the 1870s, a dynamic individual named Volsin Chiki, who would serve as chief into the 20th century, reunited the tribe and restored its pride. According to Tunica oral tradition, he refurbished the tribal cemeteries and rejuvenated ceremonies such as the Fête du Blé, or Corn Feast, thereby re-

Volsin Chiki, a Tunica leader during the late 19th and early 20th centuries, helped restore tribal pride and rejuvenate Tunica traditions.

minding the Tunica of their traditions. In 1899, a professor by the name of M. E. Chambers reported that the tribe was still "leading an agricultural life and still maintaining a tribal organization." The Tunica's consciousness of their tribal heritage was not only persisting but would flower once again in the 20th century. ▲

Rosa Jackson Pierite handweaving baskets, a traditional activity of Tunica women. This 1980 portrait was exhibited at the 1984 world's fair in New Orleans.

THE
ROAD
TO
RECOGNITION

The survival of the Tunica as a people in the 20th century is due in large part to their abiding cultural traditions, tribal structure, and system of landholding. They managed to keep much of their land because it was owned and used in common by all the tribe's members. The chief parceled out plots to individual families, periodically altering their size to take into account new family members and similar changes. Tunica hunters were free to kill game on tribal land. Certain areas, however, were specially set aside as public dance and ceremonial grounds and as family cemeteries. An expanse of land surrounding the Coulée des Grues (Bayou of Cranes) was considered sacred ground.

The tribe's communal outlook helped to preserve the tribe and its traditions. The Tunica continued to be led by a chief and to maintain their ceremonies (such as the Corn Feast), oral traditions, religious beliefs, and language. Together, these formed the core of the tribal identity.

In the early 1900s, as in earlier years, many Tunica married Indians from other tribes. In this manner the Tunica had already incorporated the Ofo and Avoyel people, as well as some Biloxi, Choctaw, and members of other Indian groups, into their tribe. Federal documents show that by 1924, Tunica leaders were formally proclaiming to the larger world their ongoing existence as a tribe. By this time, the separate cultures of the Ofo and Avoyel were little more than memories among a few Tunica families.

The Tunica had also begun to intermarry with blacks and whites. This led Ruth M. Underhill of the U.S. Bureau

An extended Tunica-Biloxi family of the early 20th century. By this time the tribe had adopted dress and housing largely similar to that of the non-Indian Louisiana community.

of Indian Affairs to pronounce in 1938 that the tribe was "too mixed to be considered Indians from a government standpoint." This was a mistaken judgment, but one that it would take decades to reverse.

In some ways, the Tunica had in fact become indistinguishable from their non-Indian neighbors. As early as 1910, photographs show Tunica people wearing clothes and living in houses similar to those found in any contemporary poor Louisiana community. Distinctively Indian dress was still worn on ceremonial occasions, however.

Some native crafts also persisted, although many of the objects the Tunica made were becoming more *pan-Indian*—similar in appearance to the work of other, unrelated tribes. Stickball was an extremely popular sport among the Tunica, and men fashioned stickball rackets from wood and made stickballs from deerhide. (Such ball games had an almost religious significance, and they have their roots in similar ball games played by tribes in the prehistoric era.)

Men also constructed ceremonial drums and the blowguns that had grad-ually come into use during the 1800s for hunting birds and small game. Collectors have found a pair of wooden figures dating from this time as well; they probably represent characters from the Tunica's ancient stories. The two figures may be horned owls; the transformation of humans into owls was a popular theme in the Tunica's oral tradition, often signifying bad luck.

The Tunica's economy reached its lowest point during the Great Depression of the 1930s. The entire country suffered in this economic crisis, but Lousiana, one of the poorest and most debt-ridden states in the Union, was particularly hard hit. Minority groups

Tunica stickball rackets. Stickball, extremely popular among tribe members, was in years past played at the end of the Fête du Blé, or Corn Feast.

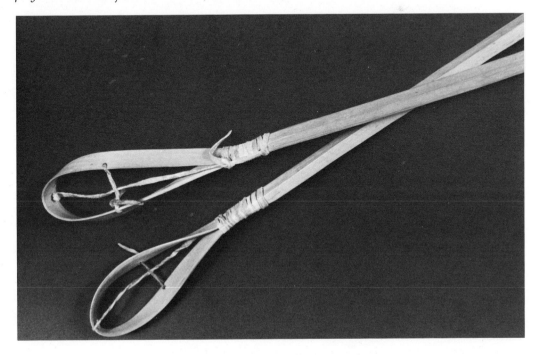

THE CORN FEAST

For countless years, the Corn Feast, or Fête du Blé, was the primary sacred ceremony of the Tunica and Biloxi tribes. Following the tribes' contact with Europeans, their sun-based theology intermingled with Christianity in a way that allowed elements of both faiths to coexist amicably, and the feast epitomizes this fusion.

By the end of the 1700s, when the Tunica settled at Avoyelles (now Marksville, Louisiana), the Corn Feast consisted of a series of rituals and events performed on sacred ground along the Coulée des Grues (Bayou of Cranes), an area comprising cemeteries, a dancing ground, and a ball field. The feast was held every summer when the corn crop was newly ripened. No one was allowed to eat any corn before the day of the feast.

The ceremony began at dawn, when families took meals of corn to the cemeteries and placed them near the headstones of graves. Men and boys then went to a particular sinkhole in the Coulée des Grues. There, facing east toward the rising sun, each either dived or was ducked into the water several times. Next the tribal chief called them individually from the water, the eldest going first. Each was given kernels of corn, which he chewed, while the chief made the sign of the cross on the celebrant's forehead. They then returned to the village.

While the men engaged in this ritual, the women and girls of the tribe prepared a variety of corn dishes. These were eaten at a midday feast. Afterward, men and occasionally women played stickball. These games were considered not simply an amusement but an inherent part of the Corn Feast.

At dusk, the community regrouped for dances. These stamping performances, often complexly choreographed, bore names such as the Coon Dance, Horse Dance, Quail Dance, and Alligator Dance. They may have honored the "animal helpers" of the tribe. The Corn Feast concluded with a final Midnight Dance.

During the 1930s and 1940s, the Tunica-Biloxi gradually stopped holding the Corn Feast but revived it in 1988. The event today serves as a reminder of both their cultural heritage and their traditional values. In the words of anthropologist H. F. ("Pete") Gregory, the Corn Feast reaffirms "connections between the living and the dead, sun and water, corn and humans, old and young. . . . All these things, seen as contrasts by Europeans, are part of an interrelated whole symbolized by the Fête du Blé."

there suffered most of all. By that time the Tunica had become essentially acculturated, but as Indians they were still discriminated against by the non-Indian population. They were disadvantaged economically, politically, and educationally. One Tunica woman, Cemonia Williams, later related of the time,

> My grandpa Eli told of when his children became five or six years old, he would take them to the school campus to enroll them in school, but . . . the white children would throw rocks at them, and forbid them to go onto the school grounds. There was a school for the blacks, a school for the whites, but there was no school for the Indians. And that is the reason that the Indians did not get an education.

During these years, many tribal members left Marksville in hopes of improving their economic prospects. Many went to Texas, where there are still a large number of Tunica. Most of these people have been absorbed into the mainstream culture.

In the 1940s, the Tunica in Louisiana lost some important facets of their heritage. Chief Sesostrie Youchigant, the last fluent speaker of the Tunica language, died. Although the language has been recorded and a few people still know isolated words and phrases, the language no longer binds the Tunica people together. In fact, it had been essentially extinct since early in the cen-

Two wooden Tunica dolls from the early 20th century. The horns may indicate that they represent humans transformed into owls, a common theme in Tunica stories, signifying bad luck.

tury, for during the last 35 years of his life Youchigant had no one with whom he could converse in Tunican.

When tribal traditionalists such as Youchigant died, they took more than language with them. The 1940s also saw

Henry Pierite (right) was among the Tunica who left the tribe's reservation in Marksville, Louisiana, for better economic opportunities. He played baseball in the city league of Houston, Texas, in the 1930s.

the last Corn Feast held by the Tunica for several decades. (The ceremony was remembered by older tribal members, however, and was finally revived in 1988.) But there are other activities now to keep the tribe united, the most important of which deal with the tribal organization and plans for the future. In religious matters, the Tunica are now part of the Louisiana Catholic mainstream, though they have retained some traditional Indian ceremonies.

Also during the 1940s, the tribe formally began a campaign to receive of-

ficial recognition of its tribal status from the federal government. This recognition would entitle them to government funding for a variety of social programs under the terms of the Indian Reorganization Act of 1934. The Tunica's battle for federal recognition would be fought by a series of chiefs, including Eli Barbry and Horace Pierite, Sr.

A second tribal campaign had its origin in the late 1960s, when a self-proclaimed treasure hunter named Leonard Charrier began to search for relics at the Trudeau site, where Tunica had lived from roughly 1731 to 1764. Charrier despoiled many Tunica grave sites, in which offerings had been deposited, and in doing so amassed the large and diverse collection of 18th-century European and Tunica artifacts now known as the Tunica Treasure. Tribal members were understandably outraged. Charrier contended that he owned objects he had removed from an abandoned cemetery. The Tunica people felt he had pilfered tribal heirlooms, and a legal contest for possession of the artifacts ensued.

The last chief of the Tunica, Joseph Alcide Pierite, Sr., died in 1976. A farmer, fishing guide, tanner, carver, stickball player, and tribal activist, he was buried in a manner that reflected the old and new ways of the tribe. Chief Joe, as he was known, was interred within the tribe's commonly owned land near Marksville, at the family plot next to his home. His grave was an aboveground crypt, common among the Louisiana French, but his head was placed toward the east, according to Tunica tradition. An electric light was installed over the grave to light the way for the deceased; this practice harks back to the ancient Tunica custom of lighting fires over tribal graves. Finally, a peace pipe, a beaded eagle feather, and other objects were also placed in the coffin.

Before his death, Chief Joe had seen the ancient chieftaincy abolished. Since 1974, when the tribe incorporated itself as the Tunica-Biloxi Indian Tribe of Louisiana, the Tunica have been led by a tribal council headed by a chairman—another step in the long road toward state and federal recognition. The tribal chairman and council continue to exercise influence over the Tunica's commonly owned land.

The following year, the state of Louisiana at last accorded the Tunica-Biloxi formal recognition, and the U.S. government followed suit in 1981. After decades of legal battle, the Tunica had proven that from early historical times they had been a distinct Indian group and had maintained their political, ethnic, and cultural integrity. One Tunica man, Harry Broussard, noted afterward, "We had a hard time being recognized. . . . And just think, we were known to the Europeans in 1541. Long time ago."

In October 1986, the U.S. First Circuit Court of Appeals upheld a lower court decision that the Tunica-Biloxi were in fact the rightful owners of the Tunica Treaure. Indeed, its existence had given substance to the tribe's claim

A photograph from the 1940s of Chief Sesostrie Youchigant, the last fluent speaker of the Tunica language.

for federal recognition, by archaeologically demonstrating the Tunica's cultural continuity. The collection was slated to be stored temporarily at the Louisiana State Museum in New Orleans, for eventual transfer to a museum to be built at the Tunica-Biloxi's Marksville home.

The tribe began to see the fruits of its long labors during the 1970s, when it constructed recreational facilities and a tribal center on its land. The federal funds the Tunica have received since acheiving recognition have further accelerated the tribe's renewal and growth. The reservation now includes a Tribal Multipurpose Building, which houses services for health care, education, job training, employment assistance, and various programs sponsored by the federal government.

The Tunica-Biloxi are still looking forward and are intent on retaining their independence. Tribal chairman Earl Barbry, Sr., asked in 1987,

> How can we really believe that we have and enjoy . . . autonomy, as long as we are dependent on federal funding for our very existence? . . .

Joseph Pierite, Sr.—known as ''Chief Joe''—was the last chief of the Tunica. He served from 1955 to 1975, at which time the position of chief was supplanted by a tribal chairmanship.

The Tunica-Biloxi's tribal center at Marksville, Louisiana. Since achieving federal recognition in 1981, the Tunica have sought to gain economic self-sufficiency by encouraging businesses to locate their operations on tribal grounds.

We should strive to become self-sufficient. This is why our tribal government has been and is continuously seeking viable businesses to enter into, or some industry to locate on the reservation. . . . This will provide employment and revenue for the tribe . . . [and] then we can truly say that we are a sovereign nation.

The Tunica today are moving confidently into a new era. By reasserting their identity, they have once again gained control over their destiny. Their optimism was expressed by Chief Joe when, shortly before his death, he said, "We have a promise from the sun. As long as there is the sun, there will be Indian people here." ▲

BIBLIOGRAPHY

Brain, Jeffrey P. *On the Tunica Trail.* Baton Rouge: State of Louisiana, Archaeological Survey and Antiquities Commission, Anthropological Study No. 1, 1988.

———. *Tunica Archaeology.* Cambridge: Papers of the Peabody Museum of Archaeology and Ethnology, Harvard University, No. 78, 1988.

———. *Tunica Treasure.* Cambridge: Papers of the Peabody Museum of Archaeology and Ethnology, Harvard University, No. 71, 1979.

Brown, Ian W. *The Role of Salt in Eastern North American Prehistory.* Baton Rouge: State of Louisiana, Archaeological Survey and Antiquities Commission, Anthropological Study No. 3, 1988.

Downs, Ernest C. "The Struggle of the Louisiana Tunica Indians for Recognition." In *Southeastern Indians Since the Removal Era,* ed. Walter L. Williams. Athens: The University of Georgia Press, 1979.

Haas, Mary R. *Tunica Texts.* Berkeley: University of California Press, 1950.

Swanton, John R. *The Indians of the Southeastern United States.* Washington, DC: American Bureau of Ethnology, Bulletin 137, 1946.

———. *Indian Tribes of the Lower Mississippi Valley and Adjacent Coast of the Gulf of Mexico.* Washington, DC: American Bureau of Ethnology, Bulletin 43, 1911.

Truex, Faye, and Patricia Q. Foster, eds. *The Tunica-Biloxi Tribe: Its Culture and People.* Marksville: The Tunica-Biloxi Indians of Louisiana, 1987.

THE TUNICA-BILOXI AT A GLANCE

TRIBE *Tunica-Biloxi (includes remnants of several other tribes, including the Avoyel, the Ofo, and the Choctaw)*

CULTURE AREA *Southeast*

GEOGRAPHY *lower Mississippi River valley of Mississippi and Louisiana*

LINGUISTIC FAMILY *Tunican (extinct)*

CURRENT POPULATION *approximately 200*

FIRST CONTACT *Hernando de Soto, Spanish, 1541*

FEDERAL STATUS *recognized; reservation in Marksville, Louisiana*

GLOSSARY

acculturation The process by which the members of a minority culture change and adapt themselves to the styles, customs, and rules of the cultural group in power.

adze An axelike stone implement used for shaping and smoothing timbers.

agriculture Intensive cultivation of tracts of land, sometimes using draft animals and heavy plowing equipment. Agriculture requires a largely nonnomadic way of life.

anthropology The study of the physical, social, and historical characteristics of human beings.

archaeology The recovery and reconstruction of human ways of life through the study of material culture (including tools, clothing, and food and human remains).

artifact Any object made by human beings, such as a tool, garment, dwelling, or ornament; also, any marking in or on the earth indicating the previous existence of such an object.

cacique The term used by the Spanish to denote an Indian chief. The Spanish learned this term from the Arawak Indians of the Caribbean with whom Columbus came into contact.

conquistador The Spanish word for "conqueror." The term used to describe the Spaniards who came to North America in the 16th century and claimed in the name of Spain lands inhabited by the Indians of the region.

culture The learned behavior of humans; nonbiological, socially taught activities; the way of life of a group of people.

earthwork Burial mound, temple mound, or other large structure built of earth. Most prehistoric earthworks in North America are found in the eastern woodlands and the prairies.

Fête du Blé A traditional Tunica feast, during which the Indians celebrated the ripening of the first corn crop. After the arrival of European missionaries, the Tunica incorporated elements of Christianity into their traditional worship of the sun-god. Events held during the feast included the placement of various corn dishes on ancestral graves, ritual observations, dances, and stickball games. In 1988, the Fête du Blé was revived after several decades of disuse.

Indian Reorganization Act (IRA) The 1934 federal law that ended the policy of allotting plots of land to individual Indians and encouraged the development of reservation communities. The act also provided for the creation of autonomous tribal governments.

loincloth A strip of animal skin or cloth that is drawn between the legs and attached to a belt tied around the waist.

Louisiana Purchase A vast tract of land purchased by the United States from France in 1803, during Thomas Jefferson's presidency. Its boundaries were eventually defined as the Sabine, Red, and Arkansas rivers to the south, the contemporary Canadian border to the north, the Mississippi River to the east, and the Rocky Mountains to the west. Jefferson hoped to relocate Indians living east of the Mississippi River to the new territory in order to open their lands for settlement by non-Indians.

midden Site consisting of one or more refuse or garbage pits. Archaeologists use information obtained from artifacts found at these sites to reconstruct past ways of life.

missionaries Members of a religious denomination who attempt to convert nonbelievers to their faith.

mound A large earthen construction built by prehistoric American Indians as a base for a public building or to contain human graves.

Paleo-Indian period The era in North America lasting until about 10,000 years ago. At that time human subsistence involved hunting and gathering food and making specialized stone tools.

palisade Structure made of upright wooden poles, constructed around a village or other settlement to protect it from enemy attack.

piakimina Tunica name for the fruit of the persimmon tree. The Indians dried the fruits and crushed them into the flour from which they made bread. Also called *ameixas*.

Portage de la Croix The land mass created by a loop in the course of the Mississippi River, enabling water travelers to shorten their journey by several miles. In the early 1700s, the Tunica created a settlement at this strategic location, which gave the Indians control of trade along the rivers. The name of the site is French for "Way of the Cross."

Quizquiz A large settlement that was located along the lower Mississippi River in what are now Arkansas and Mississippi. The city was inhabited by the ancestors of the Tunica for several hundred years until European-introduced diseases decimated the indigenous population in the late 16th century.

removal policy U.S. federal policy, initiated in 1830 with the passage of the Indian Removal Act, calling for the sale of all Indian land in the eastern and southern United States and the migration of Indians from these areas to lands west of the Mississippi River.

reservation, reserve A tract of land retained by Indians for their own occupation and use. *Reservation* is used to describe such lands in the United States, and *reserve* is used in Canada.

territory A defined region of the United States that is not, but may become, a state. The government officials of a territory are appointed by the president, but territory residents elect their own legislature.

tribe A society consisting of several or many separate communities united by kinship, culture, and language, and other social institutions including clans, religious organizations, and warrior societies.

Tunica Treasure An extensive collection of artifacts (including pottery, jewelry, and metal goods) made by both the Tunica and European colonists. The objects, which date from the early 1600s, were buried with the Tunica dead in graves at Tunica Bayou, also known as the Trudeau Site. The artifacts were excavated in the late 1960s by a non-Indian treasure hunter who claimed them for his own but were recovered in the 1970s by the Tunica-Biloxi tribe through legal actions.

wattle and daub A technique of house construction by which poles and sticks are woven together to form a frame and are then covered by mud plaster to make walls and a roof.

INDEX

PICTURE CREDITS

JEFFREY P. BRAIN is curator of Southeastern United States Archaeology at the Peabody Museum of Harvard University. He received his B.A. from Harvard University and his M.Phil. and Ph.D. at Yale University. Dr. Brain's publications include *Tunica Treasure* (1979) and *Tunica Archaeology* (1988). He has done extensive archaeological research on the Indians of the lower Mississippi River valley and was involved in the making of a documentary film on the Tunica Indians (*On The Tunica Trail*, 1978). His work has been supported by grants from many sources, including the National Science Foundation, the National Geographic Society, and the National Endowment for the Humanities.

FRANK W. PORTER III, general editor of INDIANS OF NORTH AMERICA, is director of the Chelsea House Foundation for American Indian Studies. He holds a B.A., M.A., and Ph.D. from the University of Maryland. He has done extensive research concerning the Indians of Maryland and Delaware and is the author of numerous articles on their history, archaeology, geography, and ethnography. He was formerly director of the Maryland Commission on Indian Affairs and American Indian Research and Resource Institute, Gettysburg, Pennsylvania, and he has received grants from the Delaware Humanities Forum, the Maryland Committee for the Humanities, the Ford Foundation, and the National Endowment for the Humanities, among others. Dr. Porter is the author of *The Bureau of Indian Affairs* in the Chelsea House KNOW YOUR GOVERNMENT series.